EUROPE: AN EVER CLOSER UNION

EUROPE:
an
EVER CLOSER UNION

DAVID MARTIN MEP

Vice-President of the European Parliament

SPOKESMAN
for
EUROPEAN LABOUR FORUM

First published in Great Britain in 1991 by:
Spokesman
Bertrand Russell House
Gamble Street
Nottingham, England
Tel. 0602 708318

British Library Cataloguing in Publication Data
Martin, David W.
    Europe an ever closer union. — (ELF books: 5)
    I. Title
    341.2422

ISBN 0-85124-537-4 *Cased*
ISBN 0-85124-538-2 *Paperback*

Printed by the Russell Press Ltd, Nottingham
(Tel. 0602 784505)

CONTENTS

Acknowledgements

This book expands, develops and updates a pamphlet I wrote in 1990 for the John Wheatley Centre — *European Union and the Democratic Deficit.* The additional research and much of the drafting was carried out by Colin Bartie, my Political Assistant. For this, and all the other splendid work he carries out, I am indebted.

Chapter 4 draws heavily on a paper by Drew Scott, a lecturer in the Economics of the European Community at Heriot Watt University in Edinburgh, delivered to a conference run by the Europa Institute entitled 'Beyond The Intergovernmental Conferences: European Union In The 1990s'. Chapter 9 draws on a brief prepared for the Bureau of the European Parliament's Socialist Group by Richard Corbett, a member of the Group's secretariat. I am grateful for their insights.

Finally, thanks are due to Margaret Swift, my secretary, for having personed the Edinburgh Office single handedly while the book was being written.

As always, any errors remain my responsibility.

David Martin
August 1991

Foreword

One would never guess from the newspapers, but some of the best Labour members of parliament are MEPs, Members of the European Parliament. That was not always so, naming no names — though I can say such things because I'm not running for office or seeking favour anywhere. Too old, and too unpredictable. But the new breed of Labour MEPs are good, and their colleagues in Europe obviously think so (it is the Tory MEPs who are now divided and marginalised). David Martin, for instance, is a Vice-President of the Parliament itself and is the Socialist Group's spokesperson on the European institutions. Our MEPs are perhaps good in themselves, but the job is all too real and brings out the best in people. They are where the action is, and have some influence. No longer is our group a byword for nagging foot-dragging and negative suspicion: we are now in the front of accepting the reality of greater European integration while insisting that the European Community be more directly democratic and socially responsible.

When I joined the Party in 1946 we thought of ourselves as fervid internationalists. But that was a delusion. Like the Conservatives, we suffered bad side-effects from victory in the two world wars. We vastly over-estimated Britain's strength and influence. Therefore anything the Labour Government did was internationally important. Perhaps only for the four or five immediate post-war years, we believed. True, we were genuinely anti-imperialist. But that didn't involve the movement as a whole in much knowledge of India or Africa, only a vague if passionate benevolence (what the Irish poet called 'ignorant goodwill'). It was a one-way internationalism that could end when liberation took place, and it seldom needed to listen. Otherwise internationalism was all too often, if not open fellow-travelling, at least such a euphoric hangover from the wartime alliance (when Stalin became Uncle Joe) that few Labour intellectuals were able to see as clearly as the docker from Bristol, Ernest Bevin, that it took two to divide the world into hostile armed camps. We fought German rearmament, but on the foolish ground that there was no threat and the ungenerous, almost racist, ground that Germans were inherently warlike. When Ted Heath took us into Europe, the party divided bitterly on Wilson's European referendum, indeed the referendum arose because of our divisions.

I remember the late John Mackintosh MP and I, in the Europe referendum debates, calling ourselves 'Willi Brandt socialists'. That earned us no love in Wilson's heaven. Some of us saw that the post-war Germany had broken from the past. And not just on the right of the party. More and more of the old Left found the bitter chauvinism of the opponents of 'Europe' hard to take, as Peter Shore appeared to be turning into Winston Churchill and as Tony Benn dreamt of a self-sufficient British (English?) socialist republic being a beacon light to socialists everywhere. Tom Nairn was bitingly realistic. He argued the case in an entire number of the *New Left Review* that the international nature of capitalism meant that reform in one country was impossible: 'the last fight' or the 'great compromise' (as with the Italian Communists) must be in Europe.

And now, suddenly, almost miraculously, a wider, freer Europe than even the Community opens up with the collapse of Communist power. So it is the foremost priority for the British Labour movement to consider the practical, positive use that can be made of our new standing in Europe. Europe needs us but we need Europe more. And may I make a fundamental theoretical point that effects all political thinking? Sovereignty has its limits. Harold Laski once said that 'all power is federal', or say pluralistic. Over-centralised government can actually prevent things being done. Power needs dispersing to the regions or nations-within-states who can use it most effectively, sensitively, participatively, locally. But also national governments have discovered that their power is insufficient to control, steer or even protect the market unless they pool and share some of their power. And of course this has political consequences. Of course, there cannot be the mutual benefit of a greater economic and social union without a *greater* political union; but that is a relative term, no one wants a centralised super-state. We must learn to think federally, both in the British Isles and the wider Europe as well as the European Community.

David Martin is among the most thoughtful Britons in Europe. Perhaps as a Scot he already knows that it is easily possible, indeed often enriching, to have gradated or relative allegiances, not all or nothing: Scottish *and* British, British *and* European. None of us will lose our national identities; they will simply be less attached to monopolistic and mutually hostile centralised states. David Martin has already argued powerfully, both in pamphlets and in the 'Martin Reports' of the European Parliament, about how to remedy 'the democratic deficit' in the still imperfect institutions of Europe. Now he carries the argument a stage further to show why a closer union is needed, why such a union must become more democratically accountable and why it must find a constitutional, not a treaty-bound, framework; and to ensure that its Member States do likewise. His argument is timely as well as good.

An historic sea-change of opinion is taking place among the activists of the British Labour movement. For God's sake let us put the past behind us! And, I ingratiatingly add, even ingrained foot-draggers must now take steps to be better informed (by reading what follows) if they are not to be carried away on the tide. If there is still a debate, the level has been raised. But, like David Martin, I think there is no longer a sensible 'for' or 'against' debate; only one about *how* Europe can be made more democratically effective and can best relate to Eastern Europe.

Bernard Crick

CHAPTER 1

European Union: On the Path to One World

'I am a citizen of the world.'

DIOGENES

'My country is the world and my religion is to do good.'

TOM PAINE

'I represent a party that does not exist: the party of revolution, of civilisation. This will make the 20th century. There will issue from this first the United States of Europe and then the United States of the World.'

VICTOR HUGO

It is time for European politicians to turn the poet's vision into reality. We have less than a decade left.

Although the desire for the European Community to develop into a European Union was expressed by the founding fathers of the Community, in 1952, and is explicitly stated in the first sentence of the *Preamble* to the Treaty of Rome (1957) which established a European Economic Community — 'Determined to lay the foundation of an ever closer union amongst the peoples of Europe' — it was a Member of the European Parliament, Altiero Spinelli, who gave his name to the report which led to the first Draft Treaty establishing the European Union (adopted by the European Parliament on the 14th of February 1984).

It was Spinelli himself who compared the acceptance, by the European Parliament, of this Draft Treaty on European Union to the big fish hooked by the old fisherman in the Ernest Hemingway story. By the time the fisherman gets his big prize back to the shore its carcass has been picked clean by the sharks — only the skeleton remains. I am not sure if Spinelli ever compared the Council of Ministers to a school of sharks.

Although the Single European Act (SEA), which emerged from the intergovernmental conference following adoption of the Draft Treaty on European Union, was considered by many to be a miserable fishbone, there was in fact enough flesh left on the bone to make a fish soup to whet the appetite of European parliamentarians and provide us with enough sustenance to make another sortie.

I am indeed privileged to have been handed one of the rods fashioned by Spinelli. I, like that Old Man of the Sea, have given my name to three reports (drawn up on behalf of the Committee on Institutional Affairs on the intergovernmental conferences in the context of the Parliament's strategy for European Union) known as the Martin Reports. We now have two fishes hooked to our lines: EMU (Economic and Monetary Union) and EPU (European Political Union). It is time to draw in our catch and see what we have left by the time we land these big fish on shore. Part of the purpose of this book will be to suggest what to do if our catch is once more scavenged.

Another task is to explain what is the European Parliament's strategy for achieving European Union of a federal type and in the process define that Union and its federal structure. I wish to do so in the context of what I believe to be a renewed vision of international socialism, and in the spirit of the quote from Victor Hugo.

It was on the basis of federal theory that Spinelli identified the basic contradiction of our time between the national size of political power and the internationalisation of the process of production. He imagined European Union as the first step on the way to world unification. To democratic socialists European Union is not an end in itself but a means to achieving a world union — One World — in which all people live together in harmony: giving according to their ability, receiving according to their need. European Union should be a means to an end: the bringing together of all the citizens of the world on an equal basis to participate in decisions that will sustain the earth and all its inhabitants.

As socialists we must keep in sight this ultimate goal of one world with all equal. This vision allows us to see European Union as a step on that path and prevents us from falling foul of the many possible pitfalls: constructing a fortress Europe; throwing off the concept of 'socialism in one country' only to replace it with 'socialism in one continent'; engaging in the divisive racialist debate of 'what does it mean to be European and who can join our club?'. European Union should not mean replacing British nationalism, or French, or German nationalism with European nationalism. We must expunge all chauvinism from European Union.

Some might view the foregoing declaration as an example of highblown European rhetoric: of a pragmatic Brit gone native. I believe it to be a realistic analysis of what is politically possible based on the established fact of the globalisation of capital. It is time for the European Community to take its political role in the world. I want that role to be socialist inspired.

Those who argue that the European Community is a capitalist club — always has been and always will be — are wrong. The Treaties on which the Communities are based are there to be reformed. Ultimately we must change the European Community from a Community based on treaties to a European Union with a constitution. Although entitled a 'Draft Treaty', Spinelli's document was, in fact, an embryonic constitution and, now, through a Report being prepared by Emilio Colombo, the former Italian Prime Minister, the European Parliament is preparing an updated 'Draft Constitution'.

To justify my view that the European Community is now looking beyond the narrow parameters of an economic club designed simply as a buffer to the Soviet Union, or as a trading bloc to take on the might of the Japanese and the United States of America in world markets, I ask you to compare the original *Article 2* of the Treaty establishing the European Economic Community with the suggested new *Article 2* (the first proposed amendment to the European Community Treaty in the Third Martin Report) which goes beyond involvement in domestic issues to recommend European Community engagement in: '...the harmonious and fair development of all peoples of the world to enable them to advance out of underdevelopment and hunger, and to ensure all human beings the full exercise of their political, economic and social rights'.

Of course, this is only the proposal of the European Parliament and, because we do not have a democratic Community, the word of the directly elected representatives of the people of the European Community is not *yet* law. It is this 'yet' which I find so exciting and which provides the subject matter for this book.

CHAPTER 2

European Political Union: A History, Definition and Change of Emphasis

'A map of the world that does not include Utopia is not even worth glancing at.'

OSCAR WILDE

'In Western Europe there are now only small countries — those that know it and those that don't know it yet.'

THEO LEFEVRE

I stated in chapter one that European Union has been the theoretical goal ever since the first modern conception of the European Community — a union based on consensus rather than conquest. For many, the intention was that it remained a theoretical goal to be dreamed of by poets and utopians, but never achieved.

Although the Treaty of Rome, signed in 1957, called for an 'ever closer union among the peoples of Europe', the first two decades after its signing saw little progress towards union. Indeed, General de Gaulle's opposition to majority voting in the Council and his ringing endorsement of a *'Europe des parties'*, in 1966, was a serious reversion to intergovernmentalism. As an aside, it is interesting to note that there is now majority voting in the Council of Ministers on matters connected with the Single Market, and that Mrs Thatcher's attempt to take a similar stance to de Gaulle over Economic and Monetary Union, declaring, in truly de Gaullean fashion, 'no, no, no', led to her demise rather than years of stagnation for the Community — progress indeed!

But back to history. Depressed by years of slide and stagnation, the European Community's leaders attempted in the early '80s to kick-start the Community into new life. The Stuttgart Declaration, signed by the Heads of Government at their summit there in June 1983, resolved to 'create a United Europe' and confirmed 'their commitment to ever closer union amongst the peoples and Member States of the European Community'.

Around the same time, our predecessor, Altiero Spinelli, a visionary and creative member of the Communist Group in the European Parliament, was brilliantly steering the Draft Treaty Establishing European Union through the European Parliament. Spinelli's great achievement was that he was the first politician in any of the institutions to show that a consensus could be achieved, among European political forces, in favour of creating a European Union.

Following the setting up of a Committee on Institutional Affairs in 1981, and much spade work by that Committee in the Strasbourg Parliament, the Draft Treaty was adopted by a massive majority in the plenary session of February 1984. It was immediately backed by the Belgian and Italian Parliaments and Governments, but derided by most other governments.

However, the momentum created by Spinelli's enthusiasm, and the vague, but positive, Declaration of Stuttgart, combined with the growing support for a new initiative to create a genuine 'common market', or the Single European Market as it was to be called in the coming 1992 public relations push. This led the Heads of Governments to agree, at Fontainbleau in June 1984, to establish an *ad hoc* committee to suggest how the Community could work better. The committee was led and took its name from James Dooge, a former Irish Foreign Minister. The Dooge Committee produced a list of required changes that later provided the recipe for the Single European Act.

At the Milan Summit, in June 1985, the Heads of Government decided to establish an intergovernmental conference to reform the Treaties, and consequently the Single European Act was agreed at the Luxembourg Summit in December 1985. After some difficulties with ratification, most notably the Irish Supreme Court Ruling that a referendum was required in the Republic before the government could sign the draft, the Single European Act came into force in July 1987.

Although at first greeted with despair by the supporters of the Draft Treaty on European Union, the Single European Act, with its provision for majority voting, gave new impetus towards union and effectively killed off any lingering notions of effective national vetos. It also gave new powers to the European Parliament in the legislative process, and new competences to the Community, most notably in the areas of health and safety at work, assistance to Europe's poorer regions, the environment, and research and development, as well as in European co-operation in foreign policy.

The combination of the largely unexpected impetus from the Single European Act and Jacques Delors' inspired and dynamic leadership of the Community was enough to breathe fresh life into the concept of European Union. Euro-sclerosis and pessimism gave way to new drive and optimism. However, as unexpected a bonus as its effects were, the Single Act was never going to be enough. It was an important staging post but no more than that.

Delors himself determined that the next stage must be Economic and Monetary Union. He chaired a committee of central bankers which produced a blue print for Economic and Monetary Union. At the Madrid Summit (well remembered by Mrs Thatcher, Geoffrey Howe and Nigel Lawson) in June 1989, a majority of Heads of Government voted to convene an intergovernmental conference on Economic and Monetary Union to start sometime after the summer of 1990.

It might be advisable at this stage to say a word about the importance of intergovernmental conferences (IGCs) and the consequences of the treaty reforms their decisions bring about. An intergovernmental conference (where, as the term suggests, only governments are involved) is the only mechanism whereby the treaties governing the European Communities can be reformed. Intergovernmental conferences are, by their very nature, few and far between. The Treaty of Rome setting up the European Economic Community (EEC) was, in effect, the result of· an intergovernmental conference, as was the Single European Act. Once enacted, reforms made by an intergovernmental conference cannot be changed, except by the unanimous agreement of all governments. That is why it is essential, in the short run, to make the right decisions at the two current intergovernmental conferences and, in the not too long term, to shift to a situation where Community laws can be made and reformed as a result of the expression of the popular will of a sovereign European electorate.

But back, once again, to the history. The Strasbourg Summit of 1989 confirmed the decision of the Madrid Summit and decided more specifically to hold the intergovernmental conference in December 1990 under the Italian Presidency. The European Parliament, while not hostile to Economic and Monetary Union, felt strongly that there was a need for global reform of the Treaties and could find no justification for moving forward in one sector only. Especially as this was not a sector where consensus reigned.

In a report in my name, which was adopted by a massive majority, the European Parliament demanded that the agenda of the intergovernmental conference be widened and that there should be an inter-institutional pre-conference involving the European Parliament, the Commission and Council for the purpose of preparing the mandate of the intergovernmental conference and to establish the nature of Parliament's participation in the intergovernmental conference.

Given increased significance by events in Europe, in general, and German unification, in particular, Parliament's resolution, adopted on March 14 1990, received a positive response from many quarters. On March 20 the Belgian Government issued an *aide-mémoire* supporting most of the key points in Parliament's resolution. On March 21 the Italian Parliament adopted a resolution explicitly supporting the Martin Report. Then President Mitterrand of France and Chancellor Kohl of the Federal Republic of Germany sent a joint letter to the Prime Minister of Ireland, and President in Office of the European Council, Charles Haughey. They requested that the European Council meeting, to be held in Dublin on April 25 1990, 'should initiate preparations for an Intergovernmental Conference on Political Union'. The strategy of the Council was clearly to go for two intergovernmental conferences rather than having one with a wider remit.

However, such a strategy was not the result of an aversion to Politcal Union. At a special meeting of the European Council, Council 'confirmed its commitment to Political Union' and charged the Foreign Ministers of the Member States with the task of 'preparing proposals to be discussed at the European Council in June with a view to a decision on the holding of a second intergovernmental conference to work in parallel with that on Economic and Monetary Union with a view to ratification in the same time frame'.

At the close of the Dublin Summit its host, Charles Haughey, a man not known at that time for his wild enthusiasm for things European, stated that the European Community was now 'firmly, decisively and categorically committed to European Union'. On May 17 the first meeting of the inter-institutional preparatory conference took place in Strasbourg. Discussions were positive with even the most reluctant Member State — the United Kingdom — conceding the need for some reforms to strengthen the role of the European Parliament.

The second Dublin Summit formally agreed to establish an intergovernmental conference on European Political Union. The European Parliament would have preferred a single intergovernmental conference with the agenda widened beyond Economic and Monetary Union but accepted the proposal for the two intergovernmental conferences, with the proviso that they were closely co-ordinated and were aiming for a single coherent package for ratification. Any package of reforms will have to be presented to the European Parliament and the 12 Member State Parliaments for ratification.

Assuming no major delays or hiccups, we could have a new Treaty ready for implementation on the 1st of January 1993. In other words, the goal of European Union could yet be achieved in the same time-frame as the completion of the Single Market. There is no doubt that Treaty reforms will be agreed. The only question is how bold they will be. Do our leaders have the imagination to look beyond the Single Market and create a European Community ready, willing and able to play a constructive role well into the next century?

Unfortunately, from the looks of the discussion paper delivered by the Luxembourg Presidency in April 1991 (known as the Luxembourg non-paper) and, subsequently, the Presidency's Draft Treaty of Union, the sharks are already beginning to circle. If the Treaty reforms were to be based on this document they would not come up to the Parliament's expectations. It offers less than we could possibly accept. What these documents do is simply tidy up the anomalies of the previous decade. They are not forward-looking proposals. But more of that, and what Parliament should do in response, later. It is time to state exactly what we mean by European Union, as there are many national politicians who are still confused by the concept.

Charles Haughey's remark at the Dublin Summit that the Community was now 'firmly, decisively and categorically committed to European Union' was a rather remarkable statement since Mrs Thatcher's widely reported, and much repeated, question at that meeting — 'tell me, what is Political Union?' — did not get an adequate reply from any of the other 24 participants: one Head of State, 10 Heads of Government, 11 Foreign Ministers, the Commission President plus another Commissioner.

The European Community Foreign Ministers were instructed to go away and define Political Union in time for the second Dublin Summit of 1990, to be held on June 24/25. Had there been a directly elected representative from the European Parliament present at that meeting, there would not have been such reticence, nor the need to go away and think about a definition.

The European Parliament is clear on how to define European Political Union, and has been for some time. This is not a new concept for the European Community's directly elected politicians. It refers to the same aspirations as those which lay behind Parliament's Draft Treaty on European Union of February 1984. Parliament considers the essential elements of such a union to be:

● Economic and Monetary Union with a single currency and an autonomous central bank;
● a common foreign policy, including joint consideration of the issues of peace, security and arms control;
● a completed single market with common policies in all the areas in which the economic integration and mutual

interdependence of the Member States require common action, notably to ensure economic and social cohesion and a balanced environment;

● elements of a common citizenship and a common framework for protecting basic human rights;

● an institutional system which is efficient enough to manage these responsibilities effectively and which is democratically structured, notably by giving the European Parliament the right of initiative, of co-decision with the Council on Community legislation, the right to ratify all constitutional decisions requiring the ratification of the Member States, and the right to elect the President of the Commission.

Parliament firmly believes that if these responsibilities are exercised in accordance with the principle of subsidiarity, which should be enshrined in the Treaties in such a way as to permit challenges in the Court of Justice of the European Communities — either as a precautionary step at the time of the Commission's first proposal or that of other Institutions using the power of initiative, or retrospectively by the Member States, the Community Institutions or the supreme courts of the Member States — then we will have established a practical European Union.

European parliamentarians believe if reforms are implemented which achieve these objectives, then we would have brought the European Community much closer to the European Union of a federal type as advocated in the Parliament's resolution of the 14th of March 1990, and that the next step would be to move on from a European Community based on the Treaties to one based on a constitution. Indeed the Parliament has already begun the work of drafting such a constitution — the Colombo Report — based on the Draft Treaty of European Union of 1984.

This is, perhaps, an appropriate time to explain that although European Parliamentary Reports, such as the Colombo Report and the Martin Report, are put forward in the name of the *rapporteur*, they are the property of the Parliament and subject to amendments and votes in Committee and Parliament. They need not, therefore, reflect totally the views of the person whose name they bear. Or, to put it the other way round, I do not necessarily agree with everything in the Martin Reports.

One of the principles that govern my political philosophy is the primacy of democracy. I believe democracy is about freedom and equality and fraternity; it is about the people having their say. Therefore, although I believe in Economic and Monetary Union, with a single currency and a central bank, I believe that bank should be democratically controlled. And here I come to the 'change of emphasis' mentioned in the chapter heading. Historically, it has been the case that the architects of the Community have believed in the efficacy of economic and commercial action: bring nation states together in a coal and steel agreement, set up a European Economic Community, and certain political consequences will follow. This is an example of what I believe Harold MacMillan meant when he is reported to have said 'we are all Marxists now': it is a belief that the political and social superstructure of a society would be a reflection of the economic basis. Ironically, the free-market liberal capitalists still accept this outlook when they argue that freedom and democracy are impossible without a capitalist basis, or rather that, if you introduce the market into Eastern Europe or Africa, democracy will follow. This is clearly nonsense. Democracy is the result of an act of political will and not determined by the economic basis.

In a European Community context, the argument has always been: if we were all collaborating on the management of our coal and steel industry and other commercial and economic measures we would also likely be collaborating politically and socially and not at each others throats. The rule is that political union will follow economic union as surely as night follows day.

Jacques Delors was following exactly the same principle when he convened his committee of bankers and called for an intergovernmental conference on Economic and Monetary Union. Economics is the means; politics is the end. But we have seen in Eastern Europe what happens if you follow crude economic determinism. It is time to change the emphasis and put politics first because the reality is that monetary union will lead to political union. But what kind of political union? There is no reason to believe that Economic and Monetary

Union and the completion of the Single Market will lead to democracy in the Community. I am, of course, not arguing that an autonomous European Central Bank will of itself lead to an undemocratic society — clearly, that is nonsense, as we have seen from the Federal Republic of Germany. I am arguing that you should have a democratic society that decides what the economic and political structures should be. Those structures should not be decided by bankers and bureaucrats.

In her concluding speech to the Europa Institute Conference 'Beyond The Intergovernmental Conferences: European Union In The 1990s', held in Edinburgh in April 1991, Isobel Hilton of *The Independent* suggested that it was not impossible that a version of the political union debate might have been generated by monetary union in and of itself, and then refers to a German politician who described Economic and Monetary Union as 'political union without the democracy'. This is exactly the point Parliament was making when it called for the widening of the intergovernmental conference to include, amongst other things, the addressing of the 'democratic deficit'. In a sense Council has done us a favour in splitting the original intergovernmental conference into two: Economic and Monetary Union and European Political Union. All democrats must now argue vigorously for the primacy of politics over economics. European Union should come about as a result of democratic choice and should not be economically determined. I, for one, do not want 'political union without democracy'.

Before we go on to look in detail at specific proposals to create the constituent parts of European Union, let us take a more general look at the guiding principles of democracy, subsidiarity and federalism.

CHAPTER 3

Democracy, Subsidiarity and European Union of a Federal Type

'The government of the Union, then, is emphatically and truly a government of the people. In form and in substance it emenates from them. Its powers are granted by them, and are to be exercised directly on them and for their benefit.'
JOHN MARSHALL

'Man's capacity for evil makes democracy necessary and man's capacity for good makes democracy possible.'
REINHOLD NIEBUHR

'Federal constitutions work not only because they allow for a higher degree of differentiation but because, given that you can't do away with power in any society, the ideal is to dismantle it. The criterion should be for each level of society — each city council, municipality, borough — to have as much power as it can handle. And only cede to higher levels what is strictly necessary for the conduct of business.'
HANS MAGNUS ENZENSBERGER

Events in the East have shown that, as far as the future of Europe is concerned, democracy is the key. Democracy is the safest, surest and swiftest way to achieve socialism. You can, in theory, have democracy without socialism, but you cannot have socialism without democracy. The closer you move to pure participative democracy, the closer you move to socialism.

What we must stress time and time again, in the context of an ever closer European Union, is that democracy is not about nations having a say, it is about people having a say. And that is why politicians of the right want a confederal rather than a federal European Community. The bedrock of modern European democracy is liberty, equality, fraternity. Although democrats of the right tend to stress freedom, and democrats of the left communality; equality is the linchpin. You cannot have democracy without equality: one person one vote; one vote one value. Conservatives want equality of nations; socialists want equality of people.

Many people argue, quite rightly, that you cannot have true European Union unless it is based on European culture. There is no stronger cultural basis for a European identity than a belief in democracy. Born in early Greek society, it should be the touchstone of all our political activity. Democracy is the greatest cultural contribution Europe has made to world development. The people are sovereign, the people have the right to rule.

Equally, you cannot have European Union without European public opinion. European public opinion is overwhelmingly in favour of democracy. That is why there is such an aversion to dictatorship, be it fascist or communist.

The one crucial qualification any new applicant must have to become a Member State of the European Community is that it must be a democracy. If there was nothing else in favour of the creation of the European Community, the influence it has had in making a contribution towards removing the dictatorships in Portugal and Spain and helping to bring to an end the rule of the Colonels in Greece, means that the Community has played a worthwhile role in history. Businessmen and politicians in these states knew they could never gain entrance to the European Community as long as they held out against democracy. Eastern European countries could never ever have been considered for membership as long as their leaders were in thrall of the one party state. I am fully convinced that one of the final straws that broke the back of the old communist regimes in the East was the increasing evidence of the palpable success of economies based on democracy.

It therefore remains something of an embarrassment and a cause for shame that the European Community itself is not yet a democracy properly understood; as it is not controlled by the European Community's electorate, it is not a parliamentary democracy. Indeed, if the European Community was a state and was to apply to join itself, it would be turned down on the grounds that it was not a democracy. But we are moving in the right direction and I will deal in much more detail with the mechanics of this movement in the chapter on *The New Institutional Balance*. Suffice it to say at this stage that we could not conceive of a true European Union that was not democratic. As we move towards an ever closer union we move towards an ever more democratic state.

In talking of European Union we are, by definition, talking about an extremely large political unit — one which will be playing a role in global politics and helping to pave the way to global government. Thus, we need to envisage new structures and concepts that will allow us to make some sense in talking about democracy, and, in fact, to make democracy meaningful in this context.

Subsidiarity is one such concept. One that is being increasingly used to make sense out of the practicalities of democratic government at this level. There is a fear, genuinely held by some national parliamentarians, but cynically used by those who should and do know better, that there is some kind of secret agenda to build a European superstate which will suck all power from national parliaments and control everything from a bureaucratic centre in Brussels. Nothing could be further from the truth. What European Parliamentarians want is to bring under democratic control those competencies which have already been ceded voluntarily, by the signing of Treaties, to the Community level, not to bring more power to Brussels.

The principle of subsidiarity determines that within the European Community: 'The Union shall only act to carry out those tasks which may be undertaken more effectively in common than the Member States acting separately' (notice again the stress on communal action). These tasks should be worked out in consultation and co-operation with national parliamentarians. Nothing should be done at a higher level which can be done more effectively at a lower one.

Again, subsidiarity is not a new concept for the democratically elected representatives of the people of the Community. The Parliament was at pains to give prominent and unequivocal political endorsement to the principle in the Draft Treaty establishing European Union. The principle of subsidiarity is already implicit in the Treaties and express reference is made to it there as a result of the Single European Act.

Giscard d'Estaing was the *rapporteur* on the principle of subsidiarity. As a former head of state, he is well aware of the Member States' sensibilities. The Parliament's resolution of the 12th July 1990 'on the principle of subsidiarity' acknowledges this when it states that the European Parliament has regard for 'the special nature of the Community, which is based on the principle of democracy, the precedence of Community law over national law, respect for the individual character of the Member States and a unique institutional pattern'. The resolution is also careful to state that Parliament must '...promote and safeguard the interests of all the citizens of the Union and the specific nature of the regions'.

It should be clear that with the principle of subsidiarity written into the Treaties, far-reaching competences will remain with the Member States in the fields of economics, taxation, education, culture, social security, health, family policy, the organisation of local government, public transport, infrastructure, police, penal code, private law, religion and many others. At the same time, it is essential for the creation of a European Union of a federal type that the powers already entrusted to the European Community, and the competences essential for the achievement of Economic and Monetary Union, common foreign and security policies and the establishment of a People's Europe, come under democratic control.

As a Scottish politician I am very much aware of the further possibilities of subsidiarity and federalism. I believe that power should be passed down as well as up and am very much in favour of the concept of a 'Europe of the Regions'. Jean Jacques Rousseau was one of the first European thinkers to argue for a modern concept of democracy in which all individuals should be regarded as equal in rights and should be entitled to participate in discussions and decisions which affect their lives. He believed that direct democracy was impossible in any community larger than Corsica. Whilst I believe that modern communication methods can make democracy possible in much larger units — eventually on a world scale — the concept of a Europe of the Regions holds out the exciting possibility of reinvigorating local democracy and bringing discussion and decision-making much closer to the people. That decision-making at the regional level should be linked, via a federal structure, to decision-making at the Member State and European level.

The present Member States within the European Community have become, at the same time, both too small and too large to deal effectively and democratically with geopolitical changes taking place at the global and local levels. Too small to deal with the competition from the USA and Japan, with her Pacific rim satellites, or to control the multinational companies and the globalisation of capital: hence the movement towards European Union which, due to its size and remoteness, could alienate many communities and citizens. Yet national states are too large to respond flexibly to the problems of regional imbalances and peripherality, aggravated by the creation of the European Single Market in 1992, which will suck much economic activity into a 'golden triangle' bounded by the South East of England, Northern Italy and Central Germany.

Thus a corollary to the movement towards European Union is the desire for government, and services to the citizen, to be controlled and administered as near the point of delivery as possible. This desire for democratic control to be at the lowest and most appropriate level (subsidiarity), and a strong sense of cultural identity, is manifest in many regions throughout Europe.

The desire for autonomy and increased regionalisation, which is springing up all over Europe, East and West, is the result of a great many factors, but the one common cause is the desire for self-government by communities who have a strong sense of their identity. This does not contradict the desire for movement towards an ever closer Union of the people of Europe but, in fact, grows out of it and complements it. European Union makes possible a Europe of the Regions.

I should say at this point, in order to defuse the ire of nationalists — many of whom are in favour of European

Union — by bracketing nations with regions, that by 'region' I accept the Council of Europe's definition: 'a region is a territory which constitutes, from a geographical point of view, a clear cut entity, or similar grouping of territories, whose population possesses certain shared features, and wishes to safeguard the resulting specific identity and to develop it with the object of stimulating cultural, social and economic progress'. 'Shared' features can be taken to mean language, culture, historical tradition and interests related to the economy and transport. Not all of these elements need be present in every case.

Just as the European Community's current institutional relationships and structures will be inadequate to deal with the enlargement of the Community from the outside, similarly change is needed to deal with calls for autonomy from nations and regions, which are not presently Member States, from within. What is needed is a Second Chamber of the Nations and Regions to eventually replace the Council of Ministers. This Second Chamber should be made up of representatives from national and regional parliaments. If such a Second Chamber had been in place there would have been no need for the unification of Germany, and all the concomitant fears that go with it. The five East German Länder would have joined as five regions and not as part of the largest state in the Union. If we learn from the past and look well into the future such a structure, as is envisaged in a Europe of the Regions, will be much more accommodating for the Balkans and the Baltics *et al.*

It is interesting to note that those countries, like Belgium, Spain, Italy and Germany, which are most in favour of European Union and strengthening the European Parliament, have also decentralised some of the powers of national government to their regions; whereas Britain both opposes developing the Community and devolving power and has, in fact, systematically weakened local government.

Unfortunately, we are unlikely to get a Second Chamber of the Nations and Regions from this round of Treaty reforms because of the intransigence of Member States such as the United Kingdom. The Parliament has, however, through the Martin Reports, put forward a modest proposal for the creation of a Regional Committee on the lines of the Economic and Social Committee. This would be an advisory committee comprising elected representatives of regional governments and local authorities in Member States. It would have the right to deliver opinions on regional policy and on the regional and local impact of Community policies. The proposal has won enthusiastic support from the Germans and the European Commission and, if it went ahead, would be likely to evolve out of the Commission's Consultative Council of the Regional and Local Authorities, expanding from the present 42 members, who are elected representatives, to 155 members (24 from the United Kingdom). These members would be nominated, for a four-year term, by national governments following consultation with the national organisation representing local authorities. The Committee could set up specialised working groups and the Commission would consult the general Committee on all draft legislation relating to regional policies, including the regional and local effects of other Commission policies. However, this modest proposal has its enemies. It would appear that more than two hundred years after his *Discourse on Inequality* and his *Social Contract* Rousseau's ideas are considered too radical — even in his native France.

This vision of an enlarged democratic Europe of the Nations and Regions is also motivated by a desire to make sure that the 1992 project should not lead to a 'fortress Europe'. Nor should the European Community become a massive free-market playground for multinational companies. What we in the European Parliament want is for the movement towards greater democratic control within the European Community to contribute towards the breakdown of the false barriers that have divided the peoples of East and West Europe and allowed the power blocs to exploit the Third World.

However, even if the concept of a Europe of the Regions is still controversial on the continent, federalism is not. Only in the United Kingdom do politicians, especially of the right, have a hang-up about federalism.

Federalism is the mechanism by which subsidiarity will be put into practice in a democratic European Union. Federalism is a form of government in which power is constitutionally divided between different authorities in such a way that each authority exercises responsibility for a particular set of functions and maintains its own institutions to discharge those functions. In a federal system each authority is therefore sovereign within its own sphere of responsibilities because the powers which it exercises are not delegated to it by some other authority. This appears to me to be an excellent model for the European Community and indeed for the United Kingdom.

The Labour Party in the United Kingdom is, at long last, reviving its support for federalism. Keir Hardie, one of our great founding fathers, advocated federalism. The founding programme of the Scottish Labour Party advocated Home Rule in the context of an 'Imperial Federation'. The appropriate section reads: 'Home rule for each separate nationality or country in the British Empire, with an Imperial Parliament for Imperial affairs'. Hardie carried the Imperial Home Rule model on to the British political stage when he advocated it in his election address as Independent Labour candidate for West Ham South in 1890.

Labour's new policy paper 'Devolution and Democracy' correctly points out that 'Europe began the 1980s as a collection of nation states. It enters the 1990s increasingly as a Europe of the regions'. It then goes on to state that Germany's post-war federal constitution was imposed by the allies (with Labour in power in the United Kingdom) to prevent a strong unitary state emerging. That point is worth repeating for the benefit of the United Kingdom Prime Minister and Foreign Secretary — *a federal constitution was imposed on the Germans to prevent a strong unitary state emerging.* Mr Major and Mr Hurd made it very clear at the Luxembourg Summit in June 1991 that they were opposed to the word 'federal' being in the Treaty revisions that emerge from the two intergovernmental conferences. They had no objection however to 'an ever closer Union of the peoples of Europe'. If they are not federalist then what kind of unionists are they? Because that is what they have declared themselves to be — European Unionists. Let us hope that they do not want to create the kind of union in the European Community that exists in the United Kingdom. Give me federalism any day. It does *not* mean, as the Tories would have us believe, a centralised superstate. The capital city of a European Union of federal type would be much more like Berne, in the Swiss federation, than like London became in post-union Britain.

Does anybody seriously believe that Liberals have long advocated federalism for the United Kingdom because they want a centralised superstate run from Westminster? Labour's commitment to a Scottish Parliament and Assemblies for Wales and the English regions, and the reform of the House of Lords, is an excellent basis for a federal structure for the United Kingdom that would match and marry exactly with the Europe of the Regions evolving within the European Community and being pursued by other Member States.

CHAPTER 4

Economic and Monetary Union

'Nowadays there are huge amounts of capital moving around the world. This can have an enormous effect on exchange rates. I think it would be wise to be in a system whereby you have all the weight of Member State central banks to give governments more control over the speculative attacks on capital movements. This is not a case of giving up sovereignty because much sovereignty has already been lost to the market. It is a case of governments, collectively, gaining more influence. That is the strong socialist justification for what we are proposing.'

JOHN SMITH

One of the main reasons for socialists advocating sterling's entrance into the exchange rate mechanism (ERM) of the European monetary system (EMS) and for supporting Economic and Monetary Union is to win back a position from which capital can be controlled by elected governments. We cannot therefore agree to handing over that control to bankers in an autonomous European Central Bank as part of Economic and Monetary Union. The European Central Bank must be politically accountable.

But we are jumping ahead. As we saw earlier, the European Commission, in the name of its President, Jacques Delors, decided that the next stage in the movement towards an ever closer union amongst the peoples of Europe should be Economic and Monetary Union. Delors convened a committee of bankers who drew up what is known as the Delors' Report.

The Delors' Report, presented in 1989, outlined a process for the eventual attainment of Economic and Monetary Union within the European Community. Three distinct stages in the transition were envisaged. In Stage 1 all countries would become members of the exchange rate mechanism and would restrict the movement of their currency within the 2.25 per cent band. At the same time, all exchange controls would be removed and a limited degree of reserve pooling undertaken. The Council of Economic and Finance Ministers (ECOFIN) would be responsible for overseeing monetary and fiscal (budgetary) policy developments in the 12 Member States as a precursor to the approximation of national policies envisaged during later stages in the transition to full Economic and Monetary Union. Stage two would see exchange rate adjustments becoming ever more infrequent: to be undertaken only in exceptional cases. The European System of Central Banks (commonly referred to as 'EuroFed') would be established and this would progressively take over responsibility for defining the monetary policies of individual Member States. Finally, in Stage 3, national currencies would disappear and be replaced with a single Community currency. Both domestic and international monetary policy would be conducted by the EuroFed on behalf of the Community.

The timescale for this 'staged' transition to Economic and Monetary Union was not considered by the Delors Committee. It would depend in part upon the speed at which economic convergence between the Member States was achieved, this itself being a function of the policy co-ordination conditions that would accompany each of the three stages, and the closely related matter of the institutional development of the monetary capacity at the Community level. Concrete steps have already been taken along the road to Economic and Monetary Union. Stage 1 began on the 1st of July 1990 while the Rome Summit — which spelt the beginning of the end for Mrs Thatcher — agreed that Stage 2 should begin on the 1st of January 1994. The Commission has tabled a Draft Treaty amending the Treaties establishing the European Community which contains those provisions necessary to achieve Economic and Monetary Union. It is these arrangements which are being discussed by the intergovernmental conference on Economic and Monetary Union.

Economic and Monetary Union has been a declared aim of the Community, and Member State commitment has been voiced on repeated occasions after 1969, until it was finally enshrined in the EEC Treaty by virtue of the Single Act and explicitly reaffirmed by the Hanover, Madrid and Strasbourg European Councils. Economic and Monetary Union is in a sense the logical outcome of the steps that have been taken to create a Single Market by the 31st December 1992. From this follows the need for a single currency because you cannot have a genuine Single Market without a single currency. It has been clear for some time now to socialists and federalists that no Member State of the European Community, acting alone, can provide the wealth that will be necessary in the coming decades to maintain and improve the standard of living of our people and provide the social services, security, pensions, and so on that make ours a civilised society; not to mention the resources that will be needed to help our neighbours in Eastern Europe and the peoples of the Third World. That is why countries such as Sweden and Norway are now keen to join the European Community.

However, Economic and Monetary Union will have some specific micro- and macro-economic outcomes that might do damage as well as benefit individuals and sectional interests within the Community. It should be a political matter as to how these outcomes are managed. As believers in democracy we know that the discussions and decisions should involve and be made by the people of the Community: as socialists we argue that they should be managed in favour of all the people.

As far as the micro-economic impact of Economic and Monetary Union on the Community is concerned, there is a general consensus that it will be positive. This conclusion is based on what has become the received wisdom on Economic and Monetary Union, namely that there are tangibile economic gains associated with the introduction of a single currency. These 'efficiency gains' derive from the following sources:

- the 'transactions costs' — savings that the single currency generates;
- the elimination of exchange rate uncertainty;
- further dynamic benefits due to the impact on domestic investment of an overall reduction in uncertainty.

At the same time, the introduction of a single currency is seen as an important, if not essential, accompaniment to the completion of the Single Market. As the Commission has stressed on many occasions, the economic gains potentially on offer from the Single Market will only be realised in full with the advent of a single currency. By implication, these economic gains are not as readily available in the event of a common — as opposed to a single — currency option. The United Kingdom proposal for a 'hard' ECU is really a non-starter and was already rejected several years ago when it was proposed originally by the Germans.

The macro-economic impact of Economic and Monetary Union on the Community and some of its citizens might not be quite so beneficial, unless certain policies such as a co-operative growth strategy, enhanced regional aid and direct budgetary transfers are put into operation first or at the same time.

The move to a single currency would be accompanied by the transfer of all responsibility for the conduct of national monetary policies to a 'single' Community Central Bank. In practice, the 'single' bank will be a federation of the present national central banks and is likely to work in a manner similar to the federal reserve system that operates in the USA.

There are three immediate consequences for macro-economic policy from Economic and Monetary Union. First, national authorities will lose control over domestic monetary policy. Decisions relating to money supply and, by implication, interest rates will be taken at the Community level and not at the level of the nation state. Secondly, as the Community moves towards Economic and Monetary Union, the exchange rate will increasingly become redundant as an instrument of economic policy. In the final stage, where a single currency replaces national currencies, exchange rate changes *de facto* are impossible. Thirdly, the loss of monetary policy as an instrument of national economic management necessarily places a greater burden for achieving national objectives on fiscal policy.

It is also likely, as pointed out by Drew Scott, one of Scotland's leading economic commentators on the European Community, that the transition to Economic and Monetary Union will induce some loss of sensitivity to regional problems. In short, the costs of a fixed exchange rate that presently appear at the national level will, with Economic and Monetary Union, appear as a regional problem inside a much larger system. Consequently, the urgency with which the problem would be addressed at a national level may well be replaced by a less urgent response at the Community level. This is, of course, a powerful argument in favour of a Second Chamber of the Regions administering a greatly enhanced regional fund.

One of the pressing problems that must be established before Economic and Monetary Union can go ahead is that of democratic accountability. The Bundesbank, for example, has stated quite clearly that it will only sanction a move to Economic and Monetary Union and a single European Community bank provided there are 'contractual arrangements (including binding rules and sanctions) for ensuring effective budgetary discipline in all Member States'. The Bundesbank fears that otherwise a number of Member States will be able to run substantial budget deficits that could increase the inflationary pressures for the Community as a whole. The British Labour Party has rightly questioned the right of an autonomous EuroFed having sole access to monetary policy-making, including the ability to impose sanctions on spendthrift countries. One way round this problem would be for the EuroFed to be accountable to a reformed EcoFin working in conjunction with the European Parliament. If this was the case, it would be probable that the common monetary policy would be decided in the light of the fiscal needs of the respective Member States on the one hand, balanced by the general good of all the people of the European Community on the other.

A more radical socialist proposal has recently been tabled by the Spanish. This provides for the introduction of a 'financial mechanism' to facilitate automatic fiscal transfers from the richer to the poorer countries with the advent of Economic and Monetary Union. Here the richer countries would help bring their poorer neighbours up to their level. If we could achieve this we surely would have a European Union worthy of the name. If we cannot get agreement on this, or on the British Labour Party's proposal, I fear we are heading for a multi-stage Economic and Monetary Union with those capable of moving to a 'hard' Economic and Monetary Union doing so quickly and those not yet ready or willing to join attempting to do so at a later date.

It is generally agreed that a prior condition for transition to Economic and Monetary Union must be a significant degree of convergence between the European Community Member States. In other words, were inflation rates across the European Community not to come more closely into line with each other, then the substitution of a single currency for the existing 12 national currencies would inevitably provoke a fall in output and accompanying rise in unemployment in the high inflation countries. This is what is happening at the moment in the United Kingdom because the Conservative Government took us into the exchange rate mechanism at the wrong time, at the wrong rate and for the wrong reason — short-term political expediency. The loss of the exchange rate as an instrument of policy will only be acceptable provided that either economic convergence has proceeded to an acceptable degree, or, alternatively, the adjustment mechanisms are fully in place whereby losers from Economic and Monetary Union may be assisted by the lower inflation countries that stand to gain most from a single currency Community.

As mentioned earlier, the question of greater economic convergence as a precondition for movement to a single currency was explicitly written in to the Single European Act under the general heading of 'Economic and Social Cohesion'. However, as a member of the European Parliament, my perception of what is involved in economic and social cohesion goes much wider than convergence of inflation rates and involves a much more positive political programme (such as the one I put forward in my Fabian pamphlet *Bringing Common Sense to the Common Market: A Left Agenda for Europe*) including a co-operative growth strategy and greatly enhanced regional policy. We should also look at the Community's budget: both its size and distribution. The European Community's budget is only just over 1% of the combined gross domestic products of the Twelve Member States, with the lion's share of that tiny proportion going on agriculture. The MacDougall report of 1977 argued that pre-federal integration should be backed by a European Community budget equivalent to 2-3% of combined Community GDP: Economic and Monetary Union would require 5-7%. An increase in the budget and a redistribution towards social and regional priorities would ease the path and obviate the need for multi-speed Economic and Monetary Union — in which there would be little chance of the United Kingdom being in the core group.

It is therefore in our interest to argue in favour of measures to bring about a comprehensive convergence which would facilitate the introduction of a single currency and all its economic advantages. A single currency would also facilitate making direct comparisons of wage levels and social benefits in the Member States. This in itself would be a further stimulus towards social cohesion. Which brings us to the next component of European Union.

CHAPTER 5

Turning the Common Market into a European Community

'Compassion is not a sloppy, sentimental feeling for people who are underprivileged or sick...it is an absolutely practical belief that, regardless of a person's background, ability or ability to pay, they should be provided with the best that society has to offer.'

NEIL KINNOCK

'There can be no Europe without a social dimension...1992 is much more than a creation of an internal market abolishing barriers to the free movement of goods, services and investment. The internal market should be designed to benefit each and every citizen of the Community.'

JACQUES DELORS

The task facing European socialists is to turn a Common Market, created to benefit big business, into a true European Community for all our people. It is clear to any economist that Economic and Monetary Union cannot be achieved by Member States acting separately. It is even more clear to socialists that Economic and Monetary Union will not be a success without its creation being balanced by social and environmental policies initiated in their own right. In order to achieve European Union we must ensure the Community sets high social standards, so that everyone benefits from the creation of the Single Market in 1992. But it is not just socialists who understand this. There is a remarkable consensus, even amongst politicians of the right, on the continent that we must build a social Europe. However, much of the motivation is not magnanimous but simply designed to make sure that the European Single Market is a success. Europe's Business Magazine *International Management* put it most succinctly on the front page of its September 1988 issue '1992 — The

Bad News: *Business shakeouts *Worsening unemployment *Growing trade deficits *Power shift to Brussels *Rich get richer, poor get poorer' and followed up with a series of 'bad news' headlines predicted for 1992.

Amongst the predictions were:

JOB LOSSES — As industry restructures to confront the open market, jobs will decline by between 250,000 and 500,000 before they begin to rise again sometime around 1994 and 1995.

LABOUR UNREST — With declining jobs a new era of labour conflict could begin if European Community governments don't involve trade unions in the 1992 process.

ECONOMIC DISRUPTION — While some countries may enjoy huge economic benefits once the 1992 vision is realised, even the most successful will suffer wrenching changes. For instance, some analysts believe 1992 will spell the end of the French machine tool industry.

TROJAN HORSES — While 1992 should make European industry far more competitive, it will not end the US and Japanese challenge. The IBMs and the Sonys of this world are likely to be among the leading beneficiaries of the Single Market as their European counterparts struggle to adjust.

TRADE DEFICITS — If Europe's trade balance with the United States and Japan deteriorates during the initial stages of 1992, as many economists expect, protectionism will mount.

SOCIAL POLARISATION — Despite the doubling of the European Community's budget for assisting poorer countries and regions in their efforts to catch up, few believe the Single Market will prevent a further widening of the gap between rich and poor. There are already signs that may be occurring.

POLITICAL EXTREMISM — The pain of reaching 1992 could give xenophobic movements new appeal if governments do not attach a social dimension to the Single Market's exclusively business orientation.

NO PAIN, NO GAIN — The completion of the Internal Market and managing the pain of getting there will almost certainly require a greater sharing of sovereignty among Member States. Many Europeans may find such a move intolerable.

So the message to European business is clear: 'if you want to achieve and benefit from the Single Market you will have to introduce a social dimension to the 1992 programme'.

Policies introduced to mitigate the worst effects of deregulation, policies used to bring about the Single Market, cannot be legitimately described as a social policy worth the name. None the less, despite the cynical motivation behind much of the desire to create a social Europe, we must be pragmatic enough to realise that it offers us more, in the United Kingdom, than is available from our government's domestic social agenda.

The Single European Act introduced three new elements whose purpose was to resolve the social problems connected with the completion of the Single Market:

● *Article 118 A* concerns the harmonisation of measures to improve conditions as regards the health and safety of workers. This harmonisation, which should be achieved by means of directives, must not prevent any Member State from maintaining or introducing more stringent protection measures;

● *Article 118 B* is aimed at greater dialogue between management and labour. This article's position in the Single European Act suggests that minimum measures for the health and safety of workers might be taken by means of legislation whilst any further measures would be the result of social dialogue, which, of course, is not restricted to the area of health and safety;

● the third instrument is connected with the achievement of economic and social cohesion throughout the Community by reducing the disparities between various regions and the backwardness of the least-favoured regions. The revision of the European structural funds (regional, social and agricultural) are intended to achieve this aim.

To refer to these provisions as the Community's social policy — such is the title used in the Single European Act — is overstatement, particularly when one considers that since the 1980s the Community has constantly stressed the need to establish a 'European social area' so as to give a 'social dimension' to the Single Market. However, the European Parliament has endeavoured to give fresh impetus to discussions on the social dimension, which has been given too little emphasis, by combining it with ideas for a co-operative growth strategy, increased regional funds and direct budgetary transfers.

The notion of a social dimension was given a fresh boost when the Commission, in 1989, introduced a draft Community Charter of Social Rights, which had 33 points, backed up by an Action Programme containing 45 proposals; 17 of which involved bringing forward new Directives.

Perhaps the most frustrating act of 1989, and the one that now motivates many socialists to bring about the democratic reform of the Community, was Mrs Thatcher's single-handed scuppering of the Social Charter. She was able to remove any legal basis from the Social Charter because European Community social legislation requires unanimity. Despite the fact that 11 of the 12 Member States were in favour of the Social Charter, because Mrs Thatcher was ideologically opposed to it, in European Community terms, it could become no more than a declaration by 11 governments. It might be a good idea to remind ourselves at this juncture what the Socialist Group of the European Parliament, the largest group at Strasbourg, were demanding from the Social Charter (see next page).

If we had a Community in which the European Community citizens, through their democratically elected representatives, passed the legislation, we would now be enacting the Social Charter. Because we do not have a democratic structure, one politician was able to hold up progress.

Mrs Thatcher was able to veto the Social Charter because, although the Single Act made it possible to pass measures which help to create the Single Market in the Council of Ministers by a qualified majority (54 votes out of 76 — Member States are given voting strength relative to their population size), social measures still require unanimous votes. If we are to ensure the balanced development of the Community, the social and environmental provisions of the Treaties should be among those in which majority voting in the Council also applies. This is one of the fundamental demands of the Martin Reports and its realisation would alone be a great victory for the citizens of the Community.

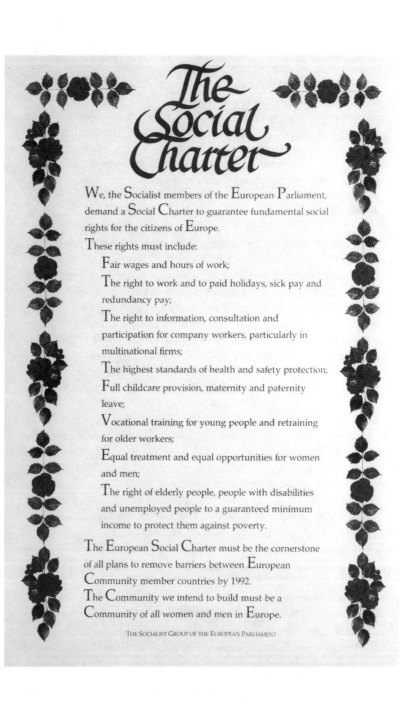

The Social Charter

We, the Socialist members of the European Parliament, demand a Social Charter to guarantee fundamental social rights for the citizens of Europe.

These rights must include:

Fair wages and hours of work;

The right to work and to paid holidays, sick pay and redundancy pay;

The right to information, consultation and participation for company workers, particularly in multinational firms;

The highest standards of health and safety protection;

Full childcare provision, maternity and paternity leave;

Vocational training for young people and retraining for older workers;

Equal treatment and equal opportunities for women and men;

The right of elderly people, people with disabilities and unemployed people to a guaranteed minimum income to protect them against poverty.

The European Social Charter must be the cornerstone of all plans to remove barriers between European Community member countries by 1992.

The Community we intend to build must be a Community of all women and men in Europe.

THE SOCIALIST GROUP OF THE EUROPEAN PARLIAMENT

The European Parliament is adamant the Single Market cannot work on free market principles alone. 'Thatcherism' has lost the battle in the Community; in fact it never really crossed the Channel. It was an offshore phenomenon of 'little Englanderism', as the political consensus in Scotland has proved at repeated general elections — the Scottish people are much more in harmony with the mainstream on the continent.

A Single Market without internal barriers cannot operate without a common approach to all those areas in which it is necessary, or desirable, for public authorities to set the rules for, or intervene in, the market. This is all the more the case if there is monetary union. These areas include:

● policies for economic and social cohesion to ensure equitable distribution of the benefits of the market;
● social policy to ensure that there is no competitive undermining of minimum standards of health, safety, working practices and social benefits;
● genuine competition policy to prevent the market being dominated by monopolies or cartels;
● harmonisation of taxation, notably indirect taxation, insofar as is necessary to prevent distortion of competition;
● common rules for consumer protection;
● common rules for the protection of the environment;
● harmonisation of some aspects of company law and banking legislation;
● common principles for direct public intervention in particular sectors such as agriculture, energy, transport, research, and so on.

Of course, the existing Treaties include some provision relating to all of these areas. The difficulty lies in the fact that the means granted by the Treaty to the Community vary considerably from one sector to another. Thus in the area of competition the Treaty gives the Commission certain powers to act directly. For consumer protection the Community can frequently act by harmonising national provisions under *Article 100A* requiring majority voting in the Council and co-operation with the Parliament. As regards the environment, or the harmonisation of indirect taxation, unanimity is required in the Council after simple consultation with the European Parliament.

These divergences are not simply a matter of concern to the elected representatives themselves: they directly affect the nature of the policy that can be carried out. Matters subject to unanimity are in fact subject to the dictatorship of the minority — as Mrs Thatcher illustrated. The Community can only go as far as its most reticent Member State will allow: this means reducing everything to the lowest common denominator. Much of this could be rectified by appropriate institutional changes, and I will deal with that in the chapter on *The New Institutional Balance.* However, the Treaty is sometimes also restrictive in its enumeration of what the Community may do in certain fields. Amongst the specific changes I would like to see implemented in order to create a social space to complement the Single Market, are:

● adding to *Article 3* of the EEC Treaty — the *Article* which sets out the activities of the Community which will bring about its fundamental objectives — the objective of common action in the field of social affairs and employment, which implies the affirmation of the right of workers to be informed and consulted before any decision affecting them is taken;

● deleting paragraph 2 of *Article 100a* EEC and including social protection along with 'health, safety, environmental protection and consumer protection' in paragraph 3;

● adding to *Article 8a* EEC that the completion and further evolution of the Single Market necessarily implies provisions to secure the convergence, at a higher level, of living and working conditions;

● adding to *Article 101* EEC the possibility of Commission intervention in cases where Community action in Member States causes serious economic or social distortion or where the intervention of the structural funds is insufficient;

● adding to the objectives of *Article 117* EEC, improved training and working conditions, equal opportunities, and access to education and culture, granted to all persons resident in the Community;

● adding to *Article 118A* EEC the harmonisation of living standards and social provision, training, minimum levels of social security and welfare, minimum provision for union law and collective bargaining;

● establishing, through *Article 128* EEC a common policy providing for all persons in the Community to have access to appropriate vocational training throughout their working life;

● modifying the last words of *Article 130a* EEC, which deals with the European Regional Development Fund, to refer to least-favoured regions and population groups.

If these specific changes were written into the Treaties as a result of the intergovernmental conferences they would go a long way to creating a genuine 'social area' to complement the Single Market and reintroduce much of the Social Charter Mrs Thatcher believed she had banished from the Community forever. There would be a clear majority for such measures within the European Parliament.

On environmental issues, it is something of a cliché to say that wind, rain and pollution know no national boundaries, but it is no less true for that. The only way to improve and protect the environment, as all socialists know, is collectively. Environmental policies must not be allowed to be vetoed by one irresponsible government in the Council. The environmental measures within the Single European Act should be brought together to form an Environmental Charter, the implementation of which should be subject to majority voting.

It is clear that if we are to achieve a European Union worthy of the name, we will require social and environmental measures that will put the European Community citizen at the centre of Community policy making. The whole purpose of European Union must be to create the good life for every individual equally. As Delors has said, we need a 'new Keynes or Beveridge' to lay down a comprehesive European Community social and employment programme for 1992, together with a plan for the redistribution of wealth.

CHAPTER 6

Fundamental Rights and Freedoms in a Citizens' Europe

'We hold these truths to be sacred and undeniable; that all men are created equal and independent, that from that equal creation they derive rights inherent and inalienable, among which are the preservation of life, and liberty and the pursuit of happiness.'

THOMAS JEFFERSON

'Every civil right grows out of a natural right; or, in other words, is a natural right exchanged...civil power properly considered as such is made up of the aggregate of that class of natural rights of man, which becomes defective in the individual in point of power, and answers not his purpose, but when collected to a focus becomes competent to the purpose of everyone.'

TOM PAINE

In order to create a citizens' Europe we must put European citizens centre stage and protect their rights collectively. The Martin Reports, therefore, have called for the incorporation into the Treaties of a slightly amended version of the Declaration of Fundamental Rights and Freedoms, originally drafted by the Belgian Member of the European Parliament, Karel De Gucht, and approved by the European Parliament on the 12th April 1989.

Parliament is quite clear that the protection of fundamental rights and freedoms must become one of the *Foundations of the Community*. Thus the new *Article 8b* would read:

1. This declaration of fundamental rights and freedoms shall afford protection for all persons in the area of application of Community law.
2. Where certain rights are set aside for Community citizens, it may be decided to extend all or part of the benefit of

these rights to other persons.

3. A Community citizen within the meaning of this Declaration shall be any person possessing the nationality of the Member States.

This would then be followed by a declaration of rights and freedoms that would define rights in such a positive way that we would begin to get an idea of the type of Community social policy that would need to be implemented in order to guarantee those rights. This would be a social policy way beyond what will be needed to ameliorate the worst effects of the creation of the Single Market. It would be a socialist social policy which would contribute towards the creation of European Union. Here is such a declaration:

Declaration of Fundamental Rights and Freedoms
General Provisions

Article 1 (Dignity)

Human dignity shall be inviolable.

Article 2 (Right to life)

Everyone shall have the right to life, liberty and security of person.

Article 3 (Equality before the law)

1. In the field of application of Community law, everyone shall be equal before the law.
2. Any discrimination on grounds such as race, colour, sex, language, religion, political or other opinions, national or social origin, association with a national minority, property, birth or other status shall be prohibited.
3. Any discrimination between Community citizens on the grounds of nationality shall be prohibited.
4. Equality must be secured between men and women before the law, particularly in the areas of work, education, the family, social welfare and training.

Article 4 (Freedom of thought)

Everyone shall have the right to freedom of thought, conscience and religion.

Article 5 (Freedom of opinion and information)

1. Everyone shall have the right to freedom of expression. This right shall include freedom of opinion and freedom to receive and impart information and ideas, particularly philosophical, political and religious.
2. Art, science and research shall be free of constraint. Academic freedom shall be respected.

Article 6 (Privacy)

1. Everyone shall have the right to respect and protection for their identity.
2. Respect for privacy and family life, reputation, the home and private correspondence shall be guaranteed.

Article 7 (Protection of family)

The family shall enjoy legal, economic and social protection.

Article 8 (Freedom of movement)

1. Community citizens shall have the right to move freely and choose their residence within Community territory. They may pursue the occupation of their choice within that territory.
2. Community citizens shall be free to leave and return to Community territory.
3. The above rights shall not be subject to any restrictions except those that are in conformity with Treaties establishing the European Communities.

Article 9 (Right of ownership)

The right of ownership shall be guaranteed. No one shall be deprived of their possessions except where deemed necessary in the public interest and in the cases and subject to the conditions provided for by law and subject to fair compensations.

Article 10 (Freedom of assembly)

Everyone shall have the right to take part in peaceful meetings and demonstrations.

Article 11 (Freedom of association)

1. Everyone shall have the right to freedom of association

including the right to form and join political parties or trade unions.

2. No one shall in their private life be required to disclose their membership of any association which is not illegal.

Article 12 (Freedom to choose an occupation)

1. Everyone shall have the right to freely choose an occupation and place of work and to pursue freely that occupation.
2. Everyone shall have the right to appropriate vocational training in accordance with their abilities and fitting them for work.
3. No one shall be arbitrarily deprived of their work and no one shall be forced to take up specific work.

Article 13 (Working conditions)

1. Everyone shall have the right to just working conditions.
2. The necessary measures shall be taken with a view to guaranteeing health and safety in the workplace and a level of remuneration which makes it possible to lead a decent life.

Article 14 (Collective social rights)

1. The right of negotiation between employers and employees shall be guaranteed.
2. The right to take collective action, including the right to strike, shall be guaranteed subject to obligations that might arise from existing laws and collective agreements.
3. Workers shall have the right to be informed regularly of the economic and financial situation of their undertaking and to be consulted on decisions likely to affect their interests.

Article 15 (Social welfare)

1. Everyone shall have the right to benefit from all the measures enabling them to enjoy the best possible state of health.
2. Workers, self-employed persons and their dependants shall have the right to social security or an equivalent system.
3. Anyone lacking sufficient resources shall have the right to social and medical assistance.
4. Those who, through no fault of their own, are unable to

house themselves adequately, shall have the right to assistance in this respect from the appropriate public authorities.

Article 16 (Right to education)

1. Everyone shall have the right to education and vocational training appropriate to their abilities.
2. There shall be freedom of education.
3. Parents shall have the right to make provision for such education in accordance with their religious and philosophical convictions.

Article 17 (Principle of democracy)

1. All public authority emanates from the people and must be exercised in accordance with the principle of the rule of law.
2. Every public authority must be directly elected or answerable to a directly elected parliament.
3. Community citizens shall have the right to take part in the election of Members of the European Parliament by free, direct and secret universal suffrage.
4. Community citizens shall have an equal right to vote and stand for elections.
5. The above rights shall not be subject to restrictions except where such restrictions are in conformity with the Treaties establishing the European Communities.

Article 18 (Right to access to information)

Everyone shall be guaranteed the right to access and the right to corrections to administrative documents and data concerning them.

Article 19 (Access to the Courts)

1. Anyone whose rights and freedoms have been infringed shall have the right to bring an action in a court of tribunal specified by law.
2. Everyone shall be entitled to have their case heard fairly, publicly and within a reasonable time limit by an independent and impartial court or tribunal established by law.
3. Access to justice shall be effective and shall involve the

provision of legal aid to those who lack sufficient resources otherwise to afford legal representation.

Article 20 (Ne bis in idem)

No one shall be tried or convicted for offences for which they have already been acquitted or convicted.

Article 21 (Non-retroactivity)

No liability shall be incurred for any act or omission to which no liability applied under the law at the time it was committed.

Article 22 (Death penalty)

The death penalty shall be abolished.

Article 23 (Right to petition)

Everyone shall have the right to address written requests or complaints to the European Parliament.

The detailed provision governing the exercise of this right shall be laid down by the European Parliament.

Article 24 (Environment and Consumer Protection)

1. The following shall form an integral part of Community policy:

● the preservation, protection and improvement of the quality of the environment

● the protection of consumers and users against the risks of damage to their health and safety and against unfair commercial transactions.

2. The Community institutions shall be required to adopt all the measures necessary for the attainment of these objectives.

FINAL PROVISIONS

Article 25 (Limits)

The rights and freedoms set out in this Declaration may be restricted within reasonable limits necessary in a democratic society only by a law which must at all events respect the substance of such rights and freedoms.

Article 26 (Degree of protection)

No provision in this Declaration shall be interpreted as restricting the protection by Community law, the law of the Member States, international law and international conventions and accords of fundamental rights and freedoms or as standing in the way of its developments.

Article 27 (Abuse of rights)

No provision in this Declaration shall be interpreted as implying any right to engage in any activity or perform in any act aimed at restricting or destroying the rights and freedoms set out therein.

The elements within the Declaration Of Fundamental Rights And Freedoms such as *Article 3* (equality before the law) which would outlaw any discrimination on grounds such as race, colour, and so on, have been greatly strengthened by the inclusion of the Declaration Against Racism And Xenophobia into the Martin Reports. In October 1990 the European Parliament voted in favour of a Report submitted by the Committee of Inquiry into Racism and Xenophobia. Amongst the 77 recommendations were:

● a European Residents' Charter to allow non-European Community nationals legally resident in a Member State the same rights on freedom of movement as European Community citizens;

● a convention on a common refugee, asylum and visa policy under European Community rather than inter-governmental auspices;

● tougher punishment, including stripping civic rights, for those convicted of racism and anti-semitism in Member States.

The Report also recommended that:

● the Legal Affairs Committee examine the possibility of Parliament taking the Council to court for its failure to respect the 1986 Joint Declaration Against Racism.

The Third Martin Report proposes to add Article 8e to the Treaty EEC which would read:

Racism and Xenophobia
The Community and its Member States, acting in these areas to which their respective authorities apply, shall take the necessary measures to avert, and where necessary to prohibit, all forms of intolerance, hostility or violence against persons or groups of persons inspired by racial, religious, cultural, linguistic, social or national differences, and to prevent any form of segregation against such persons or groups of persons.

The implementation of these two specific reforms — Declaration Of Fundamental Rights And Freedoms and Declaration Against Racism And Xenophobia — and their inclusion in the revised Treaties, following the two current intergovernmental conferences, would allow any individual who believed he or she was subject to racism in their own Member State to have the right of an ultimate appeal to the European Court of Justice.

At a time of rising racial tension within the Community it is of great importance to get these reforms implemented. Unfortunately, I am not convinced that the Member State Governments acting through the intergovernmental conferences have the political will to take on this issue. If the European Parliament, rather than the secretive Council of Ministers (or, even worse, the TREVI Group), were the law makers in this area then fundamental rights and freedoms, plus anti-racist measures, would be enshrined in European law. At the very least, the introduction of co-decision making — between the Council and Parliament — in this area would allow the Parliament to prevent the Council of Ministers bringing in 'fortress Europe' measures and reducing race relations and immigration laws to the lowest common denominator.

The struggle for democracy and fundamental rights and freedoms within the European Community are inextricably linked, and their attainment will ultimately benefit minorities and civil liberties.

The European Parliament, through the Martin Reports, has specifically called for the Court of Justice to have jurisdiction for the protection of these fundamental rights *vis-à-vis* the

Community, with the possibility of direct access to the Court of Justice for Community citizens after national appeal procedures have been exhausted. Indeed such a position might not be far away. In a front page report headed 'Historic Euro-court ruling over-rides Westminster law — and it's only the start' *The European* (July 26 - 28, 1991) declared: 'The European Court (of Justice) spelled out this week that United Kingdom Parliamentary sovereignty is over. The decision, which could open the way to millions of pounds of compensation claims by Spanish fishermen, is expected to be backed up by an even more explosive European Court decision which will give individuals the right to sue governments if they fail to put European directives into effect.'

In an article in *The Scotsman* (concerning the original ruling by the European Court of Justice following a request from the House of Lords), over a year earlier (June 21, 1990), Dr Noreen Burrows, head of the Unit of European Law at the University of Glasgow, had argued; 'There must be a strong case for re-examining the United Kingdom's position in respect of all international legal rules, not just the European Community.

'These would cover the European Convention on Human Rights and other international human rights treaties. Such an approach might solve the problem of whether to introduce a Bill of Rights in the United Kingdom or not.

'There is no logical legal reason for the United Kingdom courts accepting the supremacy of European Community law and rejecting the supremacy of the European Convention on Human Rights.'

I could not agree more. But just to take the belt and braces approach, in the Martin Reports we are suggesting that the Community as a whole should accede to the European Convention on Human Rights of the Council of Europe. This would be in order for the Community's procedures protecting fundamental rights to be subject to appeal to an external body, at least in the area covered by the Convention — in the same way as individual States, even those with charters of rights of their own, are subject to the European Convention.

In order to have a Citizens' Europe we must grant voting rights to Community citizens in municipal and European elections in their country of residence when they are not resident in their own Member State. We must also address the question of the common electoral system. The Community Treaties specify that there should be a uniform electoral procedure for European Parliament elections. Unlike other areas of Community law, where the Commission has the right to make proposals to Council, the Treaty provides in this case for the European Parliament to draw up a proposal which Council must then adopt by unanimity. Parliament made such a proposal in 1983 (The Seitlinger Report) but Council was unable to reach agreement. Parliament is now considering whether to put forward a new proposal and is due to debate the issue at one of its forthcoming sessions.

It is not just legal requirements which push the European Parliament towards making a proposal. Many Members of the European Parliament feel that having 12 different electoral systems to elect a single Parliament creates unacceptable distortions. In particular, the fact that one Member State alone does not have a system of proportional representation means that the election result in that state determines the overall political balance in the European Parliament to a greater extent than the result in any other state. To be specific, a 5% swing from right to left or vice versa in the United Kingdom will produce a shift of perhaps 20 seats, whereas in any other Member State it would produce only a 5% swing in seats. This means that, for example, the Labour Members of the Socialist Group can swing from having only 17 Members (as they did in 1979) to having 45 Members (as they do now), with only a relatively small change in the percentage vote received. In both cases Labour was the second largest Socialist Party in the European Parliament, but in one ended up being only a minor part of the Socialist Group and in the other case becoming its most important component.

The other side of the coin is the changes in the numbers of the British Conservatives, who in 1979 ended up as the largest political group in the European Parliament, despite receiving far fewer votes than the Members of some smaller groups. It is essentially unfair that the overall balance in the European Parliament depends in practice more on the election results in one Member State than in any other. The political complexion of the European Parliament should not be dependent on mid-term swings against whoever happens to be in government in one Member State.

There is, however, an argument on merit for proportional representation in European elections. Strasbourg is not a Parliament that needs a one party majority to sustain an executive emerging from the Parliament. Rather it is a reflection of the full diversity of the European Community's public opinion.

As a *quid pro quo* for the United Kingdom accepting a system of proportional representation, the other Member States should take up Bruce Millan's suggestion that any new European Community Treaty should require the use of regional rather than national lists in European elections. This would greatly facilitate the move towards a Europe of the Regions and make other Members of the European Parliament much more accountable to their electors and constituency base, thus enhancing the legitimacy of democratic representation. Such a move would also pave the way for a redistribution of seats in the European Parliament based on an equal set number of voters, rather than on the the special case of a Member State. Why should Luxembourg have 6 Members of the European Parliament for a population of half a million people when Germany has only 81 for 80 million people. Or, to put it another way, why should it take one million people to elect a Member of the European Parliament in Germany, and fewer than 100,000 to elect a similar Member in Luxembourg? Democracy is about people having a say, not nation states.

CHAPTER 7

A Common Community Foreign Policy

'We are part of the community of Europe, and we must do our duty as such.'

WILLIAM GLADSTONE

'The European Community is an economic giant but still acts like a political pygmy.'

FIRST MARTIN REPORT

The political and economic impact of the Gulf War, the problems associated with the reform process in some Eastern European countries, civil war in Yugoslavia, but, above all, the precariousness of the economic and constitutional situation in the Soviet Union make further development in Europe more uncertain than it has been since the heady days of 1989. Then it seemed possible that a peaceful order throughout Europe — a 'common European house' in the words of Mikhail Gorbachev — had become a political possibility.

What is becoming clearer and clearer is the need for the European Community to speak with one voice on foreign policy matters. The European Community must be the democratic rock, the beacon of hope, which keeps Europe stable. The Community must have the confidence in its own thinking and action both to safeguard the future democracy of its own citizens and also to provide assistance for those throughout the world, not just in the Soviet Union and Eastern Europe, who are attempting a move to democracy.

European Union needs a common foreign and security policy. But we must beware of striking off in the wrong direction. To those who see a Community security policy chiefly in terms of European participation in military operations, I would say beware of the delusion that military force is a means of achieving permanent solutions to problems. Security must not be reduced, as in current discussion, to the military level alone. Western Europe has built a peaceful order out of the ruins left after centuries of internecine enmity. We must make use of this experience to construct a new world order. The world's largest commercial power must now assume more responsibility for world politics. We cannot strive to be an economic giant and yet be content to remain a political pygmy.

With imagination and political will, we must:

● strengthen the United Nations and, with it, develop a global domestic policy for non-violent prevention of crises;
● place social justice and human dignity world-wide at the very centre of our policies;
● take disarmament seriously and control the arms trade;
● organise a dialogue between cultures and religions.

It should not be the prime task of the European Community's security policy to prepare for war in the world, but to render such wars impossible.

There has been much talk of 'the new European Community in the new world order', especially amongst our US colleagues. What will be 'new' about the European Community and what exactly is the 'new world order'? In a sense, the new European Community will be easier to define because it will evolve from the Treaty negotiation on Economic and Monetary Union and European Political Union in which the 12 Member States are currently cocooned. But what will emerge — a butterfly or a moth? The new world order, however, is a more nebulous product of President Bush's 'vision thing' — a rhetorical construct.

How can that vision be translated into reality? The new world order is generally accepted to be the notion, put forward by President Bush, of larger nations coming together under the auspices of the United Nations to stop aggression and promote the international rule of law. The United States President first articulated his vision of the new world order following a meeting with President Gorbachev in Helsinki during September 1990 in the warm after-glow following the end of the Cold War. Thus the dawn of the new world order heralded the end of the Cold War leaving the world with two dominant economies, those of the United States and Japan, together with her Pacific rim satellites. And with one political order, that of the United States.

My belief is that the process of Economic and Monetary Union will convert the bi-polar economic world of the dollar and the yen into a tri-polar one, including a single European currency. European Political Union, on the other hand, must address the question of the Community's impotence on the world's political stage. The European Community must begin to punch its political weight for the benefit of its own people and those of the Third World. European Political Union will prevent US hegemony. In political terms, the world will become bi-polar: the United States and the European Community becoming playing partners in a world game where there are many wild cards — not least of which will be the Soviet Union, or whatever takes its place.

The United States Government's opinion of the European Community is usually critical when we do not act in a united and unified way (Libya, the Gulf Crisis, and so on) and very worried if we do (Israel/Palestine, the plight of the Kurds). Much of the criticism aimed at the European Community for failure to act in a united way during the early stages of the Gulf crisis was ill-founded as the Community does not yet have an institutional mechanism to bind us by agreed collective policy. The only thing the disarray amongst the Member States highlighted was the need for a common foreign policy.

What I suspect the United States would like to hear, following the conclusion of the intergovernmental conferences, is that the European Community will introduce Treaty reforms to make us more united and financially strong enough to pick up more of the 'tab' for NATO's presence in Europe; whilst at the same time being ready to support the USA when it has to intervene — on behalf of the UN — in parts of the world where sovereignty has been abused, such as in Kuwait. In Bush's conception of the new world order the European Community would be expected to play posse to the United States as world sheriff. That is not acceptable.

Although the *realpolitik* of the new world order helped President Bush win the Gulf War, it has almost led to him losing the peace because of his failure to adequately support and defend the human rights of the Kurdish people. I believe in this, the 200th anniversary year of the publication of Tom Paine's *The Rights of Man*, the new world order must add idealism and morals to *realpolitik* if it is to gain the support of the rest of the world. The new world order must be based on peace, democracy and human rights. As Tom Paine argued, only democratic institutions can guarantee natural rights. We should be taking a much more radical approach to promoting democracy throughout the world. Perhaps we should take a tip from the old Soviet Union and export translations of Paine's *The Rights of Man*, Rousseau's *Discourse on Inequality*, and the many other works on which liberal democracy is based.

I do not believe President Bush's actions add up to a new world order at all. The bedrock of US policy is the 'inviolability of borders', as laid out for Europe in the 1975 Helsinki accords. But there are limits to the United States' emphasis on sovereignty. Mr Bush would not send troops to defend the borders of every UN member, especially those lacking oil or some other feature deemed to be vital to US interests.

The promotion of human rights is very important for ethnic, and other minorities, but it need not run counter to the US commitment to the inviolability of borders if regimes are democratic. There is a strong argument for governments to guarantee the human rights of minorities through democratic governance, within existing borders — 'pluralism not separatism' as it is described in the United States.

The promotion of democracy and the protection of human rights which may, in some cases, call for the creation of a new state need not fall foul of the Helsinki accords. These principles permit alterations of borders by peaceful, democratic means provided the host sovereign state agrees. However, for this to happen the sovereign state must be a democracy in the first place. Hence the need to promote and export democracy.

Such principles would indeed call for a 'new' European Community because the present European Community is not itself a democracy. If we are to play our part in a genuinely new world order, the European Community must get its act together and address the problem of the 'democratic deficit':

the fact that, although Member States have ceded power to the European Community, that power is not democratically controlled. Community laws are initiated by an appointed European Commission and enacted, in secret, by a Council of Ministers. The only body which is elected by the people of the European Community, on a European manifesto, is the European Parliament, which is only consulted and can be ignored. As we move towards an ever closer Union, the European Parliament must be given democratic powers.

Suffice it to say that in order for the European Community to play a greater role in the new world order it must be united and democratised. After that has been achieved, there might be an argument for the European Community itself taking a seat at the United Nations and representing Community citizens collectively. As with the European Community, could it not become a prerequisite of the new world order that members of the UN should themselves be democracies? I am sure the heirs of Tom Paine would agree.

However, we are a long way from the European Community taking up a seat in the UN. The question is how do we get to that position?

We have, in theory, already taken the first steps in formulating the mechanisms for a common European Community foreign policy. The Single European Act gave a treaty base to European Political Co-operation (EPC) — which is the name given to meetings of Member State Foreign Ministers. Nevertheless, EPC remains largely an intergovernmental matter of co-ordinating national foreign policies rather than fulfilling the stated intention of implementing 'a European foreign policy'. We must move from this loose political co-operation practised at present towards a more systematic and consistent strategy.

Paragraph 12 of *Article 3* requires Member States to examine whether any revisions of European Political Co-operation provisions are required by 1992. In the light of European and world events the answer can only be in the affirmative. The reality is that the reforms introduced by the Single European Act, in the foreign policy field, have allowed for significant but insufficient progress in this area. The progress which has been made could, however, unravel if no deeper, binding institutional commitments are made to develop and implement a common foreign policy on a permanent basis. The intergovernmental conferences should consider revising *Article 30* of the Single European Act in order to allow matters currently dealt with under European Political Co-operation to be dealt with within the Community framework.

The current division between external economic relations, which are handled by the Community's institutions, with the Commission acting as the European Community's external representative, and political co-operation, that is, foreign policy, handled by the European Political Co-operation, with the President of the European Political Co-operation acting as the European Community's external representative, is becoming more and more difficult to sustain. European Political Co-operation tends to be much slower, more cumbersome and often divisive, whereas external economic relations, such as economic aid to Eastern Europe, handled by the Commission, is more effective, swifter and much more flexible. Therefore, any genuine attempt to 'assure unity and coherence in the Community's international action' must abolish the increasingly artificial distinction between external economic relations and political co-operation.

There are several key commitments that might remove this artificial distinction and move the European Community forward in a positive way. Firstly, the Council, rather than the separate framework of foreign ministers, should be given the prime responsibility for defining foreign policy. Secondly, the European Commission should have the right of initiative in proposing policies to the Council, and also have a role in representing the Community externally, including appropriate use of its external missions in third countries. Already the 'Troika' (the present, past and future Foreign Ministers of the Council's Presidency), when visiting third countries, is normally accompanied by the responsible member of the Commission. In relation to recent events in Eastern Europe, the Commission has played a leading political role, frequently more important than the constantly — every six months — changing presidency of the European Political Co-operation. Thirdly, the functions of the European Political Co-operation secretariat should be absorbed by the Commission and Council in order to make foreign policy more clearly defined. Finally, the Community's foreign policy should be subject to scrutiny by the European Parliament in order to give it democratic legitimacy.

The European Parliament is also calling for the scope of the Community's foreign policy to include issues of security, peace and disarmament, with many in the Socialist Group, myself included, pushing for a non-nuclear defence policy for the Community. European Union could play a major historical role in the reduction of nuclear tension throughout the world. That role alone would turn the European Community into a political giant — and a gentle one at that.

The giant is also likely to get larger in the near future. Since June 1990, the European Community and the six European Free Trade Association countries (Austria, Finland, Iceland, Norway, Sweden, Switzerland) and Liechtenstein have been engaged in negotiations aimed at the creation of a European Economic Area (EEA). The United Kingdom Labour Party's Policy Review talks about supporting the entry of countries such as Austria, Norway, Switzerland and Sweden. Applications from Cyprus and Malta are in the pipeline. In the longer term it seems likely that some of the new democratic states of Eastern Europe will be in a position to put forward formal applications to join the Community, as some of their new leaders have already indicated. It is also extremely important to tie Poland, Hungary and Czechoslovakia more tightly into trade with the West by speeding up their 'association agreements' with the European Community. The European Community, along with the G7 Group of western economic leaders, must also be much more generous to the Soviet Union in order to help those dedicated to reform.

Enlargement of the Community will of course lead to logistical problems for the European Community's institutions: what is the optimum number of Members of the European Parliament?; should the system be maintained whereby the Treaty lays down the number of Members per Member State?; as far as the Presidency of the Council is concerned, can the present six month rotational Presidency be maintained when a 17 Member State European Community would lead to each state holding office only once every eight and a half years, and in the case of a 20 member European Community once every 10 years? These are very live issues that will, eventually, have to lead to a radical overhaul of the institutions. In the long run, we will have to ask far-reaching questions. Should we replace the Council of Ministers or should it be elected? Can we keep on adding to the number of European Commissioners? Should the European Parliament be sovereign? Should it be balanced in a bi-cameral system with a Second Chamber of the Regions?

In the short term, however, extending membership of the Twelve to include Eastern European countries would be difficult. It is, therefore, extremely important to strengthen other European institutions which could act as transitional mechanisms for those emergent Eastern European democracies which might eventually come into the Community's fold. The two institutions that immediately spring to mind and could, perhaps, fulfil that role are the Council of Europe and the Conference on Security and Co-operation in Europe. Indeed, the Charter of Paris has raised the Conference on Security and Co-operation in Europe to the level of a framework for the peaceful order covering Europe in its entirety. We must ensure that this process does not lose its momentum.

The Council of Europe, founded in 1949 as an international organisation bringing together 21 democratic countries of Western Europe, not only has the merit of including the 12 Member States, but shares many of the Community's aims. These include to work for closer European unity; to protect democracy and human rights; and to improve living conditions. The further expansion of the Council of Europe to include Central and Eastern European Countries would provide a new framework for co-operation in Europe. Politicians from all European countries would be able to meet and debate in a common parliamentary forum. It would give the new Eastern European democracies time to decide whether membership of the European Community was desirable for them, or whether an Eastern European Community, working closely with the European Community, might not be a better option. Recent events in the Soviet Union must make this more likely. Whatever their long-term choice, they would be able immediately to work with the Member States of the European Community in building a common European home without having to take on the rigours of full Community membership.

The first steps in this direction have already been taken. Hungary has already become a full member, whilst Poland and Yugoslavia are members of the Council for Cultural Co-operation of the Council of Europe. The USSR and Poland have 'special guest' status at its Parliamentary Assembly. Bulgaria, Poland and Czechoslovakia have applied for full membership of the Council of Europe, and the USSR has stated that it is ready for the 'widest co-operation' with it.

The new developments in Eastern Europe not only demand new political and economic responses from the European Community, but also from the USA, whose role in Europe is changing. The Conference on Security and Co-operation in Europe might provide a forum for this evolution, bringing together, among others, the USA, Canada, the European Community and the Soviet Union. It has been suggested that the Conference on Security and Co-operation in Europe should create a permanent secretariat which would be given the task of developing future co-operation.

The reform of European Political Co-operation into a common foreign policy could enable the Twelve to make a more incisive impact on the Conference on Security and Co-operation in Europe. This has been, perhaps, the most crucial forum for constructive dialogue between East and West, and has enabled millions of European citizens to restore their fundamental freedoms, which had been flouted for decades. Fifteen years after the signing of the Helsinki Final Act, many of the objectives may be said to have been fulfilled. What the emergent democracies need now is a generous European Community, speaking with a single voice, helping them to consolidate their new-found freedoms and building their own prosperity on a secure democratic foundation.

There is much debate as to whether the Community should be deepened or widened: should we put maximum effort into creating democratic union of the Twelve before we extend membership, or should we, almost immediately, extend membership to these Eastern European states requesting it? In a sense it is not an 'either, or' question. We must, of course, deepen as well as widen. Historically, widening has led to deepening. However, I am absolutely clear that we should not widen the structure on an unsafe foundation. As events are teaching us time and time again, in other parts of Europe and the world, the only basis for union is democracy — that is the bottom line. We ignore that lesson at our peril. European Union must be a democratic union or it is not worth building on.

CHAPTER 8

A New Institutional Balance

'Where does power lie...and how can it be attained by the workers?'

ANEURIN BEVAN

The quotation from Bevan's *In Place Of Fear* referred in the original text to 'this particular state of Great Britain'. By any objective criterion, whether you are in favour of it or not, power has quite clearly shifted, and is continuing to shift, to the European Community level. When Jacques Delors said that, within a decade, 80 per cent of economic and, perhaps, social legislation affecting the Member States will have its origin in the European Community, he might have got the proportion, or even the timescale, slightly wrong; but as far as the movement is concerned he was spot on. It is important to observe, however, that contrary to the impression Mrs Thatcher and her Bruges Group supporters give, the President of the European Commission was not uttering a threat but giving a warning about the way things are going, and prompting us to look at the institutional balance within the European Community.

There already exists a substantial 'democratic deficit': although a great many decisions affecting the citizens of Member States are no longer made in their national parliaments, they do not evolve from what we would understand as a democratic process at the European level.

Such a position must be of concern to all democrats but more so to democratic socialists. If we consider the quotation raised by Bevan we will see it is an extremely relevant one that all socialists must continually ask, regardless of which level they are operating at: local authority, national parliament or European Community level. To paraphrase Bevan, our task must be to ask 'Where does power lie and how can it be attained for the benefit of the people?' As democratic socialists in the Labour Party, or any of our sister Socialist Parties in the other Member States, the only way we can legitimately gain power at the European Community level is through the Socialist Group's control of the European Parliament. But the European Parliament is not in democratic control of the decision-making process of the European Community. This is the nub of our dilemma, the kernel of the problem we must solve. How can we turn the European Community into a democratic body so that, through political action, we can win a majority for our views and put them into effect at the Community level for the benefit of the people of the European Community?

I believe the problem has to be attacked on two levels. The first is through education and agitation. It is my experience that many people, especially in the United Kingdom, just do not know how undemocratic the European Community really is. They believe the Strasbourg Parliament is just like the one in Westminster; or, what is worse, they just do not care. They believe the European Community is full of meddling foreigners and the less we have to do with them the better. That will just not do because, like it or not, in or out, decisions made at the European Community level will increasingly affect all our lives. So why not try to win the support of the people to turn the decision-making process into a democratic one so that future decisions can be shaped for their benefit? Thus, the second task we must work at is the bringing forward of a set of concrete proposals for reform of the institutions of the European Community so as to get a balance more suited to the working of parliamentary democracy and open government. That is what the European Parliament has tried to do through the Martin Reports, which lay out our agenda for Treaty reforms from the current round of intergovernmental conferences. But first let me justify the claim that there is a 'democratic deficit' at the European Community level.

The democratic deficit results from the fact that powers transferred by national parliaments to the European Community are not being exercised by the democratically elected representatives of the people of the Community. We have got to say loudly and clearly to the citizens of the

European Community that there has been a loss of democracy which could, if we are not careful, facilitate a further shift towards secretive totalitarian government.

We must also scotch immediately the myth that power has shifted from Member State parliaments to the European Parliament. There is a scurrilous move afoot by those who should know better, to set national parliamentarians against European parliamentarians — a plot to divide and rule in an undemocratic manner by the corrupt status quo. The reality, as far as the European Parliament is concerned, is that over 245 million Community citizens are asked to vote every five years for a democratic fig leaf on an undemocratic system. Despite the very real changes brought about by the Single European Act — mainly to speed up the free-market aspects of the Single Market — the European Parliament is still not what we would understand as a genuine parliament: it has no power to initiate legislation or pass laws to benefit the people who voted for a particular party on a European manifesto. The Strasbourg Parliament is still, in essence, a consultative assembly. The power to make decisions lies elsewhere.

The European Community is, in fact, dominated by a sclerotic decision-making process. Its principle decision-making body, the Council of Ministers, is the only legislative (that is, law-making) body in Europe which meets in private. It is somewhat ironic that, at a time when Eastern European states are rapidly democratising, the building where the Council of Ministers meets in Brussels is referred to as 'Kremlin West'. Within the European Community, laws are made as a result of horse trading between different issues. In practice, Common Agricultural Policy decisions are swapped for budget decisions; Value Added Tax rates can be swapped for deals on harmonisation of insurance laws. It is this permanent confusion, the contrast between the bold ideas regularly reaffirmed by the Heads of Government and the sordid reality of the semi-permanent blockage, which explains and justifies public disillusionment with the European Community. The Community now needs a massive dose of democracy.

In the United Kingdom the situation in the House of Commons has become untenable. From time to time general debates on Europe are held in which details cannot be explained. On other occasions, extremely detailed points are debated in committee, or late at night, without the general approach of the Government coming under scrutiny, except when there are set piece confrontations such as the one between Geoffrey Howe and Mrs Thatcher, when personalities become more important than policies. The negotiations and implementation of the Single European Act, for example, went ahead with almost no public discussion in the United Kingdom. What a contrast with Denmark and Ireland, where the issue went to a referendum; or in France, Germany, Italy and Spain where the political leaders make European development a positive central theme in public speeches and national debate.

Notwithstanding that the standard of debate and awareness in other Member States is higher, most governments have put through their national parliaments only a fraction of the 1992 legislation agreed by the Council. In those parliaments which have voted for the legislation, there are grave misgivings by national parliamentarians. Members of the Council of Ministers appear before their national parliaments wearing their government minister's hat, presenting European legislation which national politicians have had little time to think about let alone debate, but which cannot be amended or rejected because it is the product of secret Council compromises.

But the most worrying aspect of the democratic deficit is that, under the present European Community practices, Community legislation, once accepted, not only takes precedence over national law, but can only be changed by going through the same tortuous, secretive process. What is even worse is that free-market 1992 measures, which benefit big business, can be passed by a majority vote in the Council, whereas social and environmental legislation, which benefits the people, requires unanimity.

The general problem of the relationship between the executive and the legislature in Britain is too vast to deal with here, but it is certainly clear that the development of the European Community, particularly in the foreign policy field, has increased the power of the British Government to bypass the House of Commons or, at best, to treat it as a rubber stamp. Thus, secretive, undemocratic government in the European Community is aiding secretive, undemocratic government in the United Kingdom. The problem has now become much deeper than the petty discussion about how effective Labour's front bench has been, or whether the Committee for Scrutiny of European Community legislation should have more power. If the people of the Community are to have confidence in the European Community, and if the Community itself is to become more effective, then we must put in place a more open and democratic way of making decisions.

The European Parliament, as explained earlier, has been aware of this need for a number of years. The report, prepared by the Institutional Committee, which first coined the phrase the 'democratic deficit', recognised and deplored the fact that European Community structures were developing at the 'expense of the Member States' parliaments'. The development of the Single Market in the coming years will enhance this tendency, unless something is done quickly. The Parliament's Report spoke bluntly of 'a violation of the elementary principles of democracy', pointing out that, in spite of having an elected European Parliament, 'the involvement of the people in the exercise of power...is very limited as far as Community legislation is concerned'. In short, there is a continuing transfer of power from the national to the Community level without a concomitant strengthening of democracy at that level. To achieve that end the relationship between the various Community institutions, and their relationship to the people, must be altered in order to break the corrupt status quo.

At present, the European Community is made up of four major institutions, three of which are unelected for the purpose which they serve at a European Community level. The European Commission consists of 17 politicians who are appointed under the patronage of their governments, but who swear an oath of allegiance to the Community. They run the bureaucracy and make all the proposals for legislation. The Commission's sole right to initiate legislation means that neither national nor European parliamentarians can propose legislation which would benefit their electors — we are at the mercy of the goodwill of the Commission in these matters. The Council of Ministers consists of 12 ministers, each representing their national governments, parties and parliaments, but none of whom has been elected on a European manifesto to pass European law. But these ministers are, in fact, the only people who can actually decide on legislation. Council meetings, where crucial decisions are made, are prepared by lengthy gatherings of national civil servants, whose mastery of the details of national positions and role in the implementation of European Community legislation gives them enormous uncontrolled power. These civil servants, along with their counterparts in the Commission, are the notorious 'Brussels Bureaucrats' of popular tabloid journalism. The Parliament itself consists of 518 elected politicians. They can discuss all aspects of life in the Community, and more, but, even when united, can only exert influence. Despite the fact that the Single European Act gave the Strasbourg Parliament the right to amend and to have a second reading on laws pertaining to 1992, it is still the case that legislation that has been specifically rejected by members whom the electorate have chosen to represent them at the European level, can nevertheless come into force. In a democracy, this is nothing short of scandalous, all the more so as the Council adopts legislation behind closed doors. The most powerful institution of all, the Court of Justice, which rules on the Treaties, and against whose decisions there is no appeal, is also appointed by governments. Such arrangements are in dire need of reform.

The key message which the European Parliament wishes to put across in the Martin Reports is that, above all else, the process of moving towards European Union presupposes and implies a deepening of the democratic basis on which the European Community is founded and operates. This means that the European Parliament must be made into a real legislative and monitoring body.

As the United Kingdom Government has recently been made aware, Community law is a particularly entrenched form of law. Once adopted, it cannot be amended or revoked by any national parliament, even following a general election.

Community law overrides national law. If one wants to overturn or change European Community law, the full Community procedure from Commission proposal to Council decision must be followed. It is essential, therefore, to provide for effective democratic scrutiny of the European Community generally and its legislation in particular. There is little doubt that it was this unique ability of the Community to adopt binding legislation — which means it is not a mere intergovernmental organisation — which led the founding fathers to provide for an elected parliament in the original Treaties.

The need to ensure democratic scrutiny and accountability for Community legislation existed before the 1992 programme — it was intensified by it. Any further Community competences make it an absolute imperative. Prior to the Single European Act the European Parliament had been consulted on all legislative proposals. It then gave its opinion on which the Council would make a decision, or do nothing. In some areas, to do with the Single Market, the Single European Act provided for a co-operation procedure (see figure 1) which involves two readings of the proposals by both the European Parliament and the Council, instead of the one reading under the previous consultation procedure.

A key reform would be to ensure that all Community legislation was adopted by a procedure of co-decision between the European Parliament and the Council of Ministers (see figure 2). This would mean that no piece of European legislation could be passed without the joint agreement of the Council of Ministers, representing the legitimate interests of the Member States, and the Parliament, acting on behalf of the European Community electorate as a whole. Co-decision would ensure that all Community legislation comes into force only with the approval of an elected assembly deliberating in public: this is, after all, the norm in most democracies.

Co-decision would not enable the Parliament to impose legislation which the national governments, acting through Council, were opposed to. Co-decision implies the negotiation of compromises acceptable to both sides, as in many bi-cameral systems. It would, in fact, resemble the

Figure 1

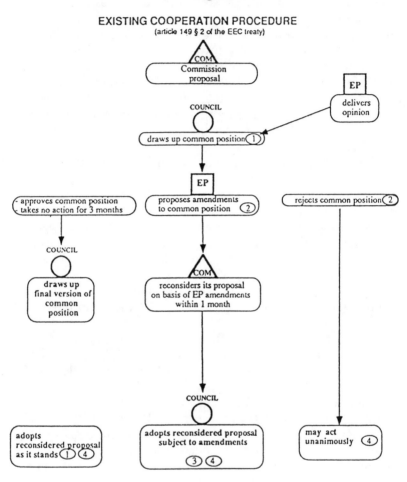

EXISTING COOPERATION PROCEDURE
(article 149 § 2 of the EEC treaty)

COM
Commission proposal

EP
delivers opinion

COUNCIL
draws up common position ①

EP

- approves common position
- takes no action for 3 months

proposes amendments to common position ②

rejects common position ②

COUNCIL
draws up final version of common position

COM
reconsiders its proposal on basis of EP amendments within 1 month

COUNCIL

adopts reconsidered proposal as it stands ① ④

adopts reconsidered proposal subject to amendments ③ ④

may act unanimously ④

end of procedure

1- qualified majority   2- absolute majority of its members
3- unanimously   4- failing a decision with one month the proposal is carried forward unadopted

Figure 2

JOINT DECISION-MAKING PROCEDURE
European Parliament proposal (to replace article 149 §2 of the EEC Treaty)

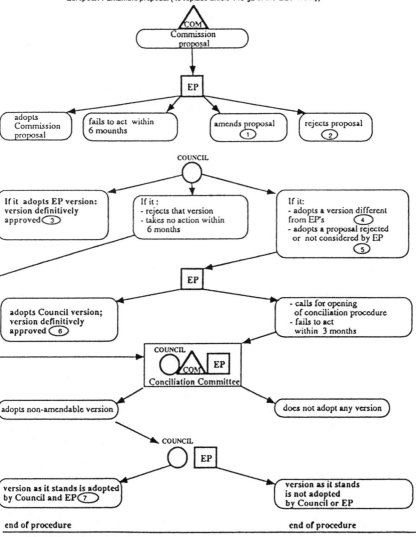

end of procedure   end of procedure

1- Amendments opposed by Commission must be adopted by majority of MEPs
2- By a majority of its Members   3- Qualified majority
4- Qualified majority- unanimously if Commission opposes amendments tabled
5- Unanimously   6- Simple majority   7- Parliament : simple majority; Council: qualified majority

institutional system that pertained in the Federal Republic of Germany between the Bundestag (elected directly) and the Bundesrat (composed of Ministers from the Land Governments and whose working methods bear a striking resemblance to those of the Council). Indeed, the conciliation procedure between the Bundestag and the Bundesrat is virtually identical to the Community's conciliation procedure. The Community's procedure should be extended to all items of Community legislation on which Council and Parliament disagree in order to make co-decision work effectively.

As mentioned earlier, the Commission is the only institution with the right to initiate proposals for legislation. The Commission's virtual monopoly on legislative initiative has not been a major problem in the past as the Commission responds quite well to suggestions made by Parliament in its own-initiative reports (about which it produces a six monthly written account of how it has responded). Parliament is now also agreeing annual legislative programmes with the Commission and this procedure could be developed further. Nevertheless, the possibility for the Commission to block an issue by refusing to make a proposal — no matter how strongly it is desired by the Parliament or Council — is potentially dangerous. The Commission is in fact able to act like a benevolent despot as far as legislative proposals are concerned.

Political parties put programmes to the people at European Elections. It is quite absurd to leave those elected with no formal means to initiate the legislative procedure required to put these programmes into action. It turns democracy into a sham. A procedure must be adopted whereby Parliament can initiate legislative proposals in cases where the Commission fails to respond within a specified deadline to a specific request, adopted by a majority of Members of Parliament.

The introduction of co-decision and the granting of the right to Parliament to initiate legislation would improve the democratic legitimacy of the Community but would still be insufficient if the Council of Ministers continued to require unanimity to approve legislation. The Single European Act did introduce the possibility of majority votes in ten new areas. However,even here, there are some national governments who claim that they have a potential right of veto that follows from the so-called Luxembourg Accords of 1966. A much more serious threat is the number of areas which still require unanimity in Council; including areas of vital importance to the Community such as social and environmental policy. Unanimity may well be justified in taking decisions that enlarge the sphere of competence of the Community, but, as this is done by Treaty amendment, unanimity is guaranteed anyway. However, unanimity cannot be justified in the management of the Community's own policies. Unanimity allows such policies to be taken hostage by individual Member States. No matter how well intentioned Member States may be, it is dangerous to give them that temptation. The possible enlargement of the Community gives further urgency to this argument.

The legislative process is, of course, only one side of Parliament's work. An equally key function for any parliament is control over the executive. In European Community terms that means the Commission.

When it comes to the appointment of the Commission, Parliament is at present consulted, through its enlarged Bureau, on the designation of the President of the Commission, pursuant to the Stuttgart Solemn Declaration on European Union of 1983. In addition, Parliament, since 1982, holds a debate and a vote of confidence on an incoming Commission when it presents itself to the Parliament for the first time with its programme. This has become an established practice and was recognised by national governments in the Stuttgart Declaration. It is significant that the two Delors' Commissions both waited until they had received the vote of confidence from Parliament before taking the oath at the Court of Justice. This practice should be formalised in any Treaty revision or new Treaty.

A more delicate question is whether the Parliament should go further and take up President Mitterrand's suggestion that the President of the Commission should be elected by the European Parliament. In its 1984 Draft Treaty *(Article 25)* Parliament drew short of making such a proposal (though it did propose that the President of the Commission, appointed by the European Council, should be free to choose the members of his team in consultation with the European Council). Fears were expressed that, if Parliament were to determine the composition of the executive then, as has happened in most national parliaments, it would become a prisoner of the executive. The majority that came together to elect a particular president would feel bound to accept her or his proposals, especially when faced with threats to resign. Party discipline would soon ensure that the European Parliament, like some other parliaments, would become a mere rubber-stamp.

I do not share these fears. The Commission's relationship to Parliament would, unless other major changes were made as well, still be some way from resembling that pertaining between the government and the parliament in certain Member States. The absence of single party majorities at European level, and the more heterogeneous nature of the party groupings that exist, mean that party discipline would be somewhat looser for many years to come. Furthermore, if the provision is maintained whereby Parliament can dismiss the Commission only by a qualified majority vote, the other political danger — that of instability — will be removed, and this will also affect the nature of the relationship between parliamentary majorities and the Commission.

The election of the President of the Commission by Parliament following each parliamentary election (that is, with a term of office of five years for the Commission to coincide with Parliament's term of office) would enable European elections to have immediate repercussions on the composition of the executive branch, just as national elections do in Member States. At present, European elections are genuinely about electing a Parliament, but the affects of casting one's vote is less immediately perceptible to the voter. To allow the Parliament to elect the President of the Commission would go some way to rectifying that situation.

A greater say for Parliament in the appointment of the Commission would almost certainly lead to it having more control over the executive, but it may not be enough. Parliament must be given 'a right of inquiry' akin to that which exists in certain national parliaments. It also requires greater control over Community expenditure, and the power to fire individual Commissioners on a two-thirds majority (at present, Parliament can only sack the whole Commission — an overly draconian measure). These powers would ensure genuine Parliamentary control over the Commission and reduce the danger of major policy decisions being taken by unelected, unaccountable and faceless Eurocrats.

There are some who, while acknowledging the existence of the democratic deficit, argue that it is not necessary to increase the powers of the European Parliament. Their solution is to strengthen the role of national parliaments. However, detailed scrutiny over Community legislation is not, generally speaking, possible to the same degree in national parliaments. National parliaments do not always have time available to spend on European proposals, and when they do it is a matter of scrutiny over their own Minister, namely one individual member of Council. In any case, he or she must be left a flexible enough position to bargain effectively. Scrutiny by twelve separate national parliaments, each over their own Minister's action, is essential but, by necessity, must be complemented by scrutiny of Council as a whole by the European Parliament. Furthermore, only the Parliament is in a position to exercise effective scrutiny and control over the Commission.

A variation on this theme has been floated by those who favour creating a European 'Senate' composed of national parliamentarians. This has two weaknesses. Firstly, the Community is already bi-cameral, with the Council of Ministers acting as a very powerful Senate. A tri-cameral system would be too cumbersome. Secondly, one has to be sceptical about the chances of recruiting able and ambitious national Members of Parliaments to such a body, and about the roles they would play once recruited. The Senators would be part-time amateurs at Strasbourg and, if they took their European responsibilities seriously, they would find it hard to maintain a profile in national politics at the same time. Therefore, we must conclude that this proposal fails to address the real issue and is simply a diversion for those who recognise the problem but are scared of the only genuine solution — real power for the democratically elected representatives of the citizens of the Community.

To answer the questions put by Bevan — where does power lie in the state and how can it be attained for the benefit of the people? — political power, at the European Community level, lies with the European Commission and the Council; economic power lies, increasingly, with multinational companies. The only legitimate way we, as democratic socialists, can attain that power for the benefit of the people is through parliamentary action. To achieve this, we need to shift the institutional balance of the European Community in favour of the democratically elected representatives of the people. (This process has similarities with the process going on in the Soviet Union.) Once the power resides where it should, with the people, it will then be possible to use the democratic process to pass legislation designed to harness the economic power of the Community for the welfare of all its people.

Of course, Bevan's questions are not yet fully applicable to the Community because the European Community is not yet a state. Therein lies part of the problem about democratic accountability. None the less, we must not wait until we get some form of European Union before we attempt to democratise it. There is no guarantee that European Union, as things stand, would be a democratic Union — that must be our greatest fear. We must use the process of working towards an ever closer Union of the peoples of Europe to build in a democratic structure to that Union. It is that process that the European Parliament, through the Martin Reports, is trying to influence.

CHAPTER 9

Proposed Treaty Reforms —
The Thin Edge of the Wedge

'Politics is the art of the possible.'
OTTO VON BISMARK

The first thing to remember when considering the effect of the European Parliament's action in favour of Treaty reforms is that the intergovernmental conferences are just that: conferences between Member State Governments. Intergovernmental conferences are the only way of reforming the Treaties and they require unanimity. That is the context in which we must place Parliament's efforts and judge our success or failure.

Although the first Martin Report requested a seat for the European Parliament at the intergovernmental conference, this was not granted. However, at the suggestion of President Mitterrand and the instigation of the Italian and European Parliaments, 'assizes'* were held which brought together parliamentarians from national parliaments and parliamentarians from the Strasbourg Parliament to discuss proposed reforms and seek common ground. There has also been a series of inter-institutional conferences, known by the French acronym CIP *(conference interinstitutionnelle parallele)*, which are meetings between the Member State Ministers involved in the intergovernmental conferences and a delegation from the European Parliament, which I have been part of. We have also been meeting individual heads of government, in their own national capitals, to put forward the views of the European Parliament, hear what their perspectives are, and see what common ground can be found.

---

* See Appendix.

Thus, the European Parliament has influence but no direct say at the meeting which will finalise the content of the new Treaty. This is likely to happen at the Maastricht summit of December 1991. The new Treaty could then be ratified by national parliaments during 1992 and signed at the Edinburgh Summit in December 1992, coming into effect on the 1st of January 1993 and coinciding with the completion of the Single Market. However, there is some danger that the Treaty will not be agreed in that time scale because of the fact that on several key points the United Kingdom is in an oppositional minority of one. Treaty reforms require unanimity. A Labour Party victory at a British general election prior to the summit in December would, of course, hasten a much more constructive outcome as Labour takes a more positive attitude on such aspects as majority voting in the Council on social and environmental issues — a sticking point for the Conservative Government.

Perhaps the strongest cards the European Parliament holds in getting its agenda accepted are its support from the Commission and certain Member States, plus its threat to refuse to co-operate . The Italian Parliament has stated that it will not ratify the new Treaty if the European Parliament does not approve it. Similar positions may be taken by the Belgian and German Parliaments. The French Parliament is pressing for a second 'assizes' at the end of the intergovernmental conferences. The European Parliament itself could threaten to veto any further accessions to the Community unless enough of its agenda is satisfied — no widening without substantial deepening.

Let us just remind ourselves what the substantive elements of the Parliament's agenda are before going on to look at the possible outcome and what Parliament's response might be. The Parliament believes that the implementation of eight clear demands would achieve European Union. Those demands are:

● economic and monetary union with a single currency and an autonomous central bank;
● majority   voting   in   the   Council   of   Ministers   on

environmental and social policy in order to achieve a more balanced Community;

● common foreign policy in order to standardise and co-ordinate European Community policy and reaction to external and world events;

● elements of common citizenship and a common framework for fundamental rights and freedoms;

● the establishment of a Regional Assembly to contribute towards and monitor policy affecting the regions of the Community;

● the right for the democratically elected representatives of the Community to initiate legislation;

● the right of the European Parliament to appoint the President of the Commission which would run for the same time span as the Parliament, thus making the executive more responsive and relevant to the people;

● the establishment of co-decision making between the European Parliament and the Council, thus ensuring that no European Community law could be passed without the joint agreement of the Council, representing the Member States, and the Parliament, representing the Community electorate as a whole.

Parliament believes that if these responsibilities are exercised in accordance with the principle of subsidiarity, then a democratic European Union will have been established.

Although at the time of writing we do not yet know exactly what will be in the final Treaty, we have been given a broad outline. Just before the Luxembourg meeting of the European Council of the 28th and 29th of June 1991, the Presidency tabled a 'Draft Treaty of Union'. This replaced its previous 'non-paper' of the 15th of April, which was the first attempt to draw together over one hundred individual proposals submitted to the intergovernmental conferences. Negotiations will be based on this new text, although revised versions will be produced in due course by the Dutch Presidency prior to the Maastricht Summit. It is now up to European parliamentarians to use the remaining time to further press their agenda through the CIP process, by influencing Member

State parliamentarians and by mobilising Community public opinion.

My initial response to both the 'non-paper' and the Council's 'Draft Treaty of Union' is that they contain more than we were originally led to expect, but less than Parliament could accept given the position laid out in the Martin Reports. In essence the Council's Draft Treaty of Union tidies up some previous anomalies left by the Single European Act but does not fundamentally advance European Union nor eliminate the democratic deficit. Indeed, in many ways, the Council's Draft Treaty of Union tips the balance further to the benefit of the Council and thus represents a step backwards to intergovernmentalism.

There is a fundamental philosophical flaw in the conception of the Council's Draft Treaty of Union in that it is not based on the idea of Union at all. I would have to agree with the Commission's written response to the 'non-paper', on the 21st of May 1991, when it said that because the Council's proposal does not seek to bring all matters within the same legal framework it is not consistent with '...the basic thinking which has been behind the construction of Europe for forty years now, namely that all progress made towards economic, monetary, social or political integration should gradually be put together in a single Community as a precursor of European Union'.

The structure put forward by the Luxembourg Presidency has been described as a 'Greek Temple' with three separate pillars: one being the European Communities; the second constructed out of common foreign and security policy; and the third consisiting of co-operation on juridical affairs. These three pillars are capped by the European Council. It is proposed that each pillar would retain its separate legal character and have different institutional provisions.

It has been observed that in some ways the fundamental structure is similar to that in the Single European Act which contained, in a single treaty, provisions amending the Community Treaties and new provisions on European Political Co-operation . The latter was to be carried out not by the Council but by 'the Foreign Ministers meeting in European political co-operation'. The Luxembourg

Presidency argues that its proposals would take this provision a stage further because European Political Co-operation would be carried out by the Council, with a role for the other Community institutions. This argument is fundamentally flawed because, legally, European Political Co-operation would remain separate and therefore not subject to control by the Court of Justice. The Council tries to argue that the new accommodation would move European Political Co-operation from being purely intergovernmental to a halfway stage towards *'Communitaurisation'.* However, we only have their word for that, because although European Political Co-operation would move into the Council, it would still not be open to the Parliament. It should also be said that there is a certain feeling of *déjà vu* about this, as the same claim was made at the time of the Single Act which formally linked European Political Co-operation to the Community, provided for Commission participation in European Political Co-operation, and a scrutiny role for Parliament, yet firmly kept the other institutions at arm's length.

If we look even closer at the Luxembourg proposals, we will see that the structure really has, at least, five pillars. The Council's Draft Treaty also provides for defence matters to be implemented through the Western European Union (WEU) — a proposal which will prove contentious. Economic and monetary union, although formally in the Community 'pillar', are to be conducted, for monetary matters, by an independent central bank and, for economic matters, by the Council assisted by a special economic and financial committee composed of representatives of Member States and taking over the traditional functions of the Commission and of COREPER (the Member States' representatives in Brussels).

The Commission has argued that if foreign and security policy were to stand alone as a pillar, fully separated from all other policies, with equal but separate status to the Community, then the objective agreed in the Rome European Council meeting of securing '...coherence of the overall external action of the Community' would be prejudiced. The 'Union' would be the entity acting externally in some areas, and the 'Community' would be the entity for other areas. This would be likely to cause confusion across the world, especially where it is difficult to draw a dividing line in such areas as arms exports, sanctions, technological aid, and so on, and inhibit the Community in acting in a coherent and comprehensive manner.

In meeting some of the objections put forward by the Commission, the Council is now exploring a possible compromise: 'pillars with bridges'. It is also attempting to meet objections that the intergovernmental conferences have lost their way, in terms of European Union, by the Presidency proposing that its Draft Treaty will have a preamble referring to the ultimate federal objective of the whole construction, and to convene a new intergovernmental conference in 1996. This has met with strong United Kingdom opposition.

The whole enterprise is beginning to remind me of a similar mock-ancient Greek structure on top of Calton Hill in Edinburgh, which was to be constructed by the City fathers in 1822 to commemorate the end of the Napoleonic Wars. It was started but never completed and is now known as 'Edinburgh's disgrace'. I am concerned that the Luxembourg Draft Treaty of Union will meet a similar fate and will become the 'Community's disgrace'.

'Pillars with bridges'? — the whole enterprise is beginning to resemble a building site full of the rubble of demolition and reconstruction. I would be much happier with an organic structure — a natural analogy — much more in harmony with the ethos of a Community moving towards an ever closer union of the peoples of Europe. We should be viewing the Community as a tree, with a main trunk and several strong limbs, branches and laterals, supporting many forms of life. Perhaps an oak tree which has grown from a small acorn, or a sturdy fruit tree with many vigorous grafts. The Community must be perceived holistically, as an organic unit which is growing. The relationship between institutions should be symbiotic rather than structural. Symbiosis — the association of two different organisms which live attached to each other and contribute to each other's support — is the essence of federalism. I am sure the citizens of the Community would rather walk through an orchard than negotiate the rubble of a building site. Trees bear fruit, Greek temples tend to crumble.

We should now perhaps look briefly at the proposals in the Council's Draft Treaty which relate to the Parliament's agenda for European Union to see how they compare, and to devise a strategy for taking our arguments further. But before we do that we should note that the Draft Treaty includes extensions to competencies within the Community's pillar to areas such as education, transport safety, industrial policy, tourism, consumer protection, public health, civil protection, culture, development, and so on, as well as reaffirming the principle of subsidiarity. The treaty would specify that, in areas that are not of its exclusive jurisdiction, the Community would only take action '...if and so far as those objectives can be better achieved by the Community than by the Member States acting separately because of the scale or effects of the proposed action'.

Dealing with the Council's proposals, in the order I have outlined, Economic and Monetary Union comes first. Technically the Intergovernmental Conference on Economic and Monetary Union is well ahead of that on European Political Union because it deals with this one issue. It was also subject to far greater preparation in the Delors Committee and elsewhere. Although I accept the fundamental logic of Economic and Monetary Union and the inevitability of a single currency — you cannot have a genuine single market without a single currency — I am still uneasy about the inherently undemocratic way it is to be managed. Even some of those in the Parliament who are in favour of an autonomous European Central Bank are unhappy with the Luxembourg proposals. They would lead to a highly independent Central Bank — even more independent than the Bundesbank — which would have full control over monetary policy. The European Bank's President would have to report to Council and to Parliament, but neither would be able to dismiss her or him, nor force a change of policy. Parliament would only be consulted on appointments made to the Executive Board, even for the President. This is not good enough. It is not even clear if the Council's economic powers would balance the Bank's monetary powers. Although there should be no interference with the day to day running of the Bank, there must be more overall democratic control over the setting and direction of policy.

Socialists must stand firm on their determination to have majority voting in the Council extended to the social and environmental fields. Here the United Kingdom Conservative Government's implacable opposition is a major stumbling block. A United Kingdom general election could, therefore, be crucial for progress in the Community. It appears that even the mild extension put forward in the Council's Luxembourg text is not acceptable to British Tories. The Draft Treaty provides for:

- Community Directives adopted by qualified majority, in co-operation with the Parliament, to lay down minimum standards for the working environment; health and safety of workers; working conditions; information and consultation of workers; equal opportunity; vocational training of persons excluded from the labour market;
- Community provisions adopted by unanimity, after consulting Parliament, on social security, social protection and employment of third country nationals;
- no Community legislation concerning pay, the right of association or the right to strike;
- consultation of workers and management by the Commission before submitting proposals. Agreements reached between management and labour at European level could be translated into community legislation.

The United Kingdom Government's categorical opposition to the widening of the definition of social policy and their opposition to any extension of majority voting could wreck the whole Single Market project, since it is not acceptable that working people alone should pay the price for restructuring.

On economic and social cohesion, the proposals from Spain to enhance this policy by budgetary transfers are meeting with strong opposition, even from the Commission. This resistance seems shortsighted because some fairly substantial measures are going to be needed if there is to be the necessary convergence to bring about Economic and Monetary Union. President Delors, however, claims that Community transfers to the two poorest Member States are actually greater than transfers within the Federal Republic of Germany to its poorest States — it is not clear if this includes the East German Länder.

Progress seems more likely on environmental matters. The current Treaty provision would be amended to provide for majority voting and co-decision with Parliament for 'multiannual action programmes setting out priority objectives', but there will be only the co-operation procedure for the rest. The division between the two is not clear as the multiannual programmes are not defined. Nevertheless, the introduction in all classes of qualified majority voting would be highly welcome. The Draft also lays down slightly clearer provisions for Community action in international frameworks. *Article 2* of the Treaty would be modified to include 'sustainable development' among the objectives of the Community.

In its proposals to the intergovernmental conferences on a common foreign policy, the Martin Report went beyond the Parliament's 1984 Draft Treaty and advocated the merging of European Political Co-operation into the Community framework, albeit with a preponderant place for Council in the decision-taking procedure. Although the Commission position is consistent with this, the Luxembourg Draft Treaty is opposed. The Council would have common foreign and security policy (CFSP) in the second 'pillar'. This second pillar in the Luxembourg text is based on current European Political Co-operation provisions but with the following changes:

● it would be the Council, not 'the Foreign Ministers in European Political Co-operation', which would be responsible for defining the Community's policy within the framework of overall guidelines laid down by the European Council. The European Political Co-operation secretariat would consequently be absorbed into the Council;
● the restriction to discussing only economic and political aspects of security would fall, but defence matters would normally be delegated to the Western European Union;
● a new Treaty revision on defence matters would take place in 1996, just before the Western European Union treaty is due to run out;

- COREPER, not the Political Committee, would prepare ministerial meetings;
- it would be possible to agree unanimously areas of 'common action' where implementing measures would be adopted by a qualified majority.

This maintenance of formal separation from the Community framework, and therefore from the external policies of the Community, on trade, research, transport, development aid, and so on, is unacceptable. So too is the fact that it would be up to the Presidency of the Council to conduct the functions of external representation, and that the Presidency should be assisted in the preparation and implementation of decisions by COREPER. If this went ahead, the CSFP, unlike the Community, would have no legal responsibility.

There is division amongst Member States on the priority they wish to give to NATO over the Community framework and the linked discussion of the role of Western European Union. There are particular problems with the military aspects of security policy for Ireland and, possibly, for some applicant states such as Austria. Concerning the stated objectives of the common foreign and security policy, the text is quite close to that proposed by the European Parliament in the Martin Reports, referring to the safeguarding of common values and interests, preserving peace and security, strengthening international peace, promoting international co-operation and consolidating democracy, the rule of law and respect for fundamental rights.

I regard the so-called third 'pillar' — juridical co-operation — in the Presidency's Draft Treaty with circumspection. It would provide a Treaty basis for the type of intergovernmental co-operation that currently takes place in frameworks such as TREVI (a secretive group of Foreign, Law and Order and Defence Ministers accountable to no-one). It would deal with matters such as external controls, visa policy, immigration, civil law and criminal matters. The Ministers would, unlike now, be required to inform the European Parliament of their activities and take its views into account, and would carry out most of its activities in the Council. Unanimity would be the general rule, but it could be agreed that certain implementing measures might be adopted by qualified majority. The Commission would have a non-exclusive right of initiative. Legal instruments would normally be in the form of international conventions requiring national ratification, but the Court of Justice would be given competence to interpret such conventions and settle differences. If this is the case, why, then, does juridical co-operation require a separate 'pillar'?

As far as aspects of common citizenship and fundamental rights and freedoms are concerned, it looks like the European Political Union intergovernmental conference is close to agreement on the granting of voting rights to Community citizens in their country of residence for local and European elections, and for consular assistants in third countries. However, the news on fundamental rights and freedoms is not so good. It is proposed that the introductory provisions of the new Treaty would provide for the Union to respect the rights and freedoms of citizens as recognised in the European Convention for the Protection of Human Rights and Fundamental Freedoms. However, placing this *Article* in the Treaty where it is proposed diminishes its legal effect as it comes in the part referring to the European Union as a whole — which has no legal personality — rather than in the Community 'pillar' where it would have had legal effect. It must be transferred.

On regional representation, the proposed Draft Treaty takes up the European Parliament's proposal to set up a body for regional and local authorities to be represented at Community level, but links it to the Economic and Social Committee. This is totally unacceptable as it joins directly elected representatives of the people with professional representatives. Regional and local authorities are totally opposed to such a set up. They need and deserve a body of their own. The Commission and the Parliament are pressing for a separate body for regional representatives. This is a proposal that has come on the agenda fairly late and has not received adequate attention. I predict that the issue of a Europe of the Regions to complement European Union and balance any tendency towards centralism will bring such a body much more prominence in the future. It will also be necessary to enhance the federal structure of the Union and to make sense of subsidiarity. In many cases it is regional and local authorities who have to carry out European Community Directives or put Community policy into practice; so it is only sensible and fair that these institutions play a more active role in framing those policies in the first place.

As far as the right for Parliament to initiate legislation is concerned, the proposed Draft Treaty only offers Parliament the ability to encourage the Commission to propose legislation. This is not good enough. Why should Community citizens take the democratic credentials of the European Community seriously if members of their Parliament cannot put a programme to them in their manifestos that they have the power to implement if they are elected?

The Draft Treaty does propose that the Parliament should be given more power over the executive by being consulted on the designation of the President of the Commission. The Parliament would also give a vote of confidence on the Commission as a whole. Although this is not exactly what the Parliament asked for — the right to elect the President — a negative opinion in the consultation on the President of the Commission is unlikely to be overridden as the candidate in question would probably not wish to proceed without the endorsement of the Parliament. It is also likely that at least one Member State would probably agree with Parliament and thus the candidate would not be appointed. Failing that, the Parliament could withhold its confidence in the Commission as a whole. In these circumstances consultation is tantamount to a confirmation or election.

Where the Draft Treaty has been petty is in not changing the term of office of the Commission from four to five years to coincide with Parliament's term of office. Such a move would have had both practical and symbolic significance for the Parliament and the Community's electors by giving the European elections a direct impact on the appointment of the European Community's executive. There must be more movement here.

Significantly, there has been most movement, in principle, on the Parliament's key demand for co-decision making procedures with the Council. The Luxembourg proposal provides for Parliament and Council to adopt a limited number of Community 'laws' by a co-decision procedure. Under the draft treaty 'laws' would be the term used for traditional regulations and directives whenever the co-decision procedure applies. The proposal envisages that co-decision would apply to:

- definition of objectives, general rules, co-ordination and organisation of the structural funds;
- the framework programme for research — which would be more detailed than at present;
- pluriannual programmes for specific domains of environmental policy;
- indicative plans (blueprints) for trans-European networks;
- development co-operation as regards multiannual programmes and as regards the rules for financial and technical co-operation and for food aid.

As to the procedure itself. As proposed by the Presidency (see figure 3) it would work like this:

- first readings in Parliament and Council as in current co-operation procedure (that is, the Commission retains discretion over accepting Parliamentary amendments, but if it accepts them Council can only modify them unanimously);
- in the second reading, Parliament will consider the Council's common position as in the current co-operation procedure except that: it can adopt amendments by simple majority; if it rejects the text, the text will fall, whereas, at present, Council can overrule Parliament's rejection by unanimity;
- Council will then vote on Parliament's amendments by a qualified majority. If it accepts all of them the text is adopted. If it doesn't, the matter is referred to conciliation;
- a conciliation committee, of 12 Member State Ministers and 12 Members of the European Parliament, has six weeks to negotiate an agreement acceptable to a qualified majority, on Council's side, and a majority, on Parliament's side. The Commission participates without the right to block decisions. If agreement is reached, Parliament, by a simple

Figure 3

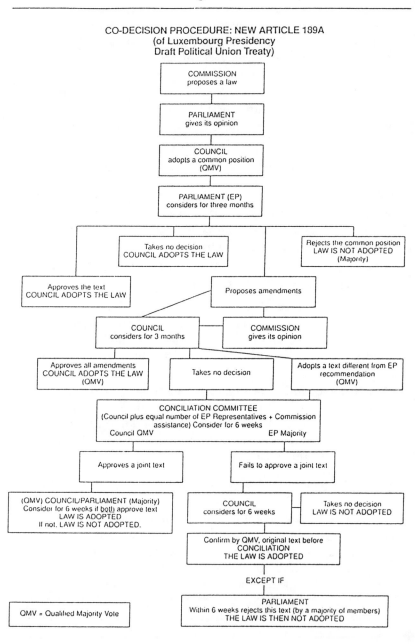

CO-DECISION PROCEDURE: NEW ARTICLE 189A
(of Luxembourg Presidency
Draft Political Union Treaty)

COMMISSION
proposes a law

PARLIAMENT
gives its opinion

COUNCIL
adopts a common position
(QMV)

PARLIAMENT (EP)
considers for three months

Takes no decision
COUNCIL ADOPTS THE LAW

Rejects the common position
LAW IS NOT ADOPTED
(Majority)

Approves the text
COUNCIL ADOPTS THE LAW

Proposes amendments

COUNCIL
considers for 3 months

COMMISSION
gives its opinion

Approves all amendments
COUNCIL ADOPTS THE LAW
(QMV)

Takes no decision

Adopts a text different from EP
recommendation
(QMV)

CONCILIATION COMMITTEE
(Council plus equal number of EP Representatives + Commission
assistance) Consider for 6 weeks
Council QMV   EP Majority

Approves a joint text

Fails to approve a joint text

(QMV) COUNCIL/PARLIAMENT (Majority)
Consider for 6 weeks if both approve text
LAW IS ADOPTED
If not, LAW IS NOT ADOPTED.

COUNCIL
considers for 6 weeks

Takes no decision
LAW IS NOT ADOPTED

Confirm by QMV, original text before
CONCILIATION
THE LAW IS ADOPTED

EXCEPT IF

QMV = Qualified Majority Vote

PARLIAMENT
Within 6 weeks rejects this text (by a majority of members)
THE LAW IS THEN NOT ADOPTED

majority, and Council by a qualified majority, must approve it;

● if conciliation fails to reach agreement, Council can adopt its text (possibly with some of Parliament's amendments) by a qualified majority, if the Commission agrees, or by unanimity, if the Commission disagrees. Parliament would then have six weeks to reject this text by a majority of its members, causing it to fall.

This procedure mainly differs from the Parliament's proposal in the Martin Report in that it maintains the Commission's rights over parliamentary amendments in the first reading, and that it provides for a procedure should conciliation fail. This allows Council to adopt its own text, challenging the Parliament to take the negative course of rejecting it. Nevertheless, it does improve on the current co-operation procedure. Whatever the Commission's views, the Parliament can force Council to consider its amendments in a second reading and, if they are not adopted, convene the conciliation committee. The strength of the Parliament's negotiating position depends on the seriousness of its threat of rejection and its ability to organise parliamentary opposition. There is, of course, inherent dangers for the Parliament in that it would be seen to be responsible for killing the legislation. However, the possibility of rejection, used carefully, is a powerful weapon. A weapon that could be clearly understood by the citizens of the Community who could be mobilised behind Parliament's position. The main drawback of this reform is not the procedure, although that could be better, but its scope — it must apply to more than a handful of measures.

Other proposals in the Presidency's Draft Treaty of Union that will affect the powers of the Parliament include the extension of the Assent Procedure. Parliament's assent would be required for an extended number of international agreements — about double the number at present covered, the uniform electoral system, *Article 235* of the EEC Treaty but not *236*, the creation of new structural funds and certain aspects of citizenship — measures to facilitate free circulation and the right of residence throughout the Community. Assent in these new areas, and those for international agreements, would now require a simple majority in Parliament instead of a majority of all Members, as is the case at present.

The Draft Treaty also proposes the extension of the co-operation procedure to several new areas:

● transport;
● various action programmes (tourism, consumer protection, public health, civil protection, development aid not covered by co-decision, education, vocational training and culture);
● inter-operability of European networks;
● loan guarantees and studies for trans-European networks;
● support measures for industry;
● energy policy;
● environmental matters not covered by co-decision.

It also seems likely that the intergovernmental conferences will put forward a clause in the Treaty to formalise the right for Parliament to set up committees of inquiry, to receive petitions and to elect an ombudsman.

That is what is on the table at the time of writing, three clear months prior to the Maastricht summit in December 1991. It is obviously well short of what the Parliament is asking for through the Martin Reports. However, there is still time for negotiation and the application of pressure, from public opinion and political parties, on Member State Governments because, at the end of the day, they are the people with the power to make the decisions.

I believe that the Socialist Group should press the Parliament to concentrate on a small number of key points. These include:

● co-decision — here we should press for the scope of the proposed procedure to be widened to cover all matters on which Council acts by a qualified majority;
● the extension of qualified majority voting in Council to environmental and social matters. Here it looks like we'll win on the environment but lose out, due to the United Kingdom's intransigent ideological opposition, on social matters. It will be extremely hard for Socialists to convince our supporters that there has been a shift from a Common Market mentality to one supporting the creation of a true

European Community for all citizens unless we win this one.

- the appointment of the Commission — we must press for this to take place after the European elections with a five-year term of office for the Commission;
- organic structure — we must argue for the re-assertion of a holistic approach to the Union, not for separate pillars — even if they do have bridges.

So what are Parliament's options if the offer on the table is not substantially better than that put forward by the Luxembourg Presidency? We could reject it and take up the Italian Parliament's offer to refuse to endorse the Treaty changes. The Strasbourg Parliament could refuse to assent to any further accessions until we got our way. I fear that neither of these courses of action is likely to win substantial progress. In the first case, the position of the Italian Parliament might have shifted by the time the new Treaty has been presented and, even if it hasn't, there is always the danger that the United Kingdom Government, for opposite reasons, might be happy to see the European and Italian Parliaments uniting to block some proposals it is uncomfortable with. The second option — Parliament refusing assent to any new accessions — also has its dangers: alienating public opinion inside the Community and building up unhelpful hostility towards the European Parliament in the states who are applying to join. I do not believe either tactic should be ruled out at this stage, but they should only be used as a last resort, after thinking through all the possible consequences.

At the end of the day, the likelihood is that, barring a general election in the United Kingdom, we are unlikely to win majority voting in the Council on social policy. Our greatest practical victory, therefore, must be seen to be winning the principle of co-decision making with the Council. The proposal for co-decision making offers our best chance to date. It must be clearly seen as the thin edge of the wedge. We must ram it home for all it's worth. If Parliament is hard working, disciplined and astute we can use what is on offer to tilt the institutional balance in favour of democracy and continue our battle to wrest political power for the citizens of the Community.

CHAPTER 10

One Small Step

'An invasion of armies can be resisted, but not an idea whose time has come.'

VICTOR HUGO

There is nothing as powerful as an idea whose time has come. The people of Eastern Europe know that. John Major and other members of the Council of Ministers cannot continue to call for democracy in the Soviet Union and deny it to the citizens of the European Community. Democracy is an indivisible concept. The rulers of the European Community must be called to account at Maastricht. To use Major's analogy, the genie is out of the bottle; the reform process is underway, it cannot be reversed.

As far as the Socialist Parties, in general, and the British Labour Party, in particular, are concerned, a democratic European Union is the big idea that must be grasped and promoted with enthusiasm. Only European Union can provide the basis which will allow us to take the same qualitative leap, in terms of social provision for our people, that the Labour Party took in the United Kingdom in 1945.

The left in Europe, but especially in the United Kingdom, must restore their nerve and confidence. In a sense we have been startled and stalled, like a political rabbit, in a set of ideological headlights: one beam of which was the glare from the collapse of Soviet socialist systems in the East; the other was from Mrs Thatcher's torching of the socialist superstate.

Let's stop defending, pretending and apologising and go on the offensive. Let's not be frightened of words and let's not fall into the trap of accepting our opponents' definitions. A socialist superstate is exactly what we do want to create: if by socialist superstate we mean a state that above all delivers the good life to all our people. Individual Member States can no longer individually deliver the social provision and equality we all want; it now needs to be achieved collectively through European Union.

Be clear about one thing. If we do not create a socialist superstate we will end up with a capitalist superstate where we are all slaves of the market. Who wants to end up like the United States of America where poverty still persists in a land of plenty? We are at a crossroads, we have an opportunity that will never come again. We can either take the American way or forge ahead with a distinctly European programme.

The earlier discussion about democracy, subsidiarity and federalism should have made it clear that what is being proposed is not the centralised bureaucracy, based in Brussels, of Mrs Thatcher's demonology. Rather, it is a federal system that allows us to pool our resources, to create wealth and use collective mechanisms to re-distribute that wealth, whilst, at the same time, re-invigorating democracy through a Europe of the Regions that begins to realise Rousseau's dream of participative democracy. There will, of course, have to be an increased emphasis on education. Education is vital for any extension of democracy.

Many people have commented on the fact that the recent momentous events in the Soviet Union, which have overthrown the Revolution of 1917, have in a sense allowed Russia to return to the real social democratic revolution that was hijacked by Lenin's Bolshevik Party. This is true, of course, but it is just as true that events in the Soviet Union at the turn of the century also hijacked the left for Marxist socialism. There were many other strands of utopian socialism which were silenced by Marxism/Leninism. These, I predict, will see a revival. We have not witnessed the end of socialism but its rebirth.

Let us also be clear that in moving towards an ever closer Union of the peoples of Europe we are categorically not attempting to create identikit Europeans. The last thing I want to replace British, or French, or German nationalism with is European nationalism — although I would be much happier humming Ode To Joy than God Save the Queen. The project is much smaller and much larger. It is about basing government on the individual and creating World Union. As modest as it has been, the development of the European

Community towards European Union has been one of the great success stories of the 20th century. So let us start to proclaim it as such. We could be providing a model for others in Africa, in Central and South America, in Asia, and so on. That model must be a democratic one.

Although the Soviet Union is falling apart, and the United States is experiencing great social strain as a result of substantial ethnic minorities not sharing in the fruits of the 'American dream', the European Community's slow, painstaking, consensual approach towards Union is working, and does hold out hope for the future. If the people of a continent that was the cockpit for two major wars this century can work together in shared institutions that allow them to speak together in their own languages to find a common way forward, then there is hope for other areas of the world that are experiencing major conflicts.

But we are not moving fast enough on the democratic front in the Community. All the progress that has been made could be wrecked unless it is placed on a democratic foundation. One thing that must be learnt from history is that only democracy, and the ability of the people to replace their government, provides the safety valve necessary for peaceful progress. With the European Community now a major player, or stumbling block, in the world trade (GATT) talks,and the possibility of future trade wars with the United States of America and Japan, the people doing the negotiating for the European Community must have a democratic mandate. They must be responsible to the citizens of the Community, not to powerful interest groups. It is that democratic accountability that the European Parliament is trying to achieve through the agenda it set out, for the intergovernmental conferences, in the Martin Reports

If I was asked how should the citizens of the Community judge the results of the integovernmental conferences, I would have to say 'democracy is the key'. Anything that increases and enhances democracy must be considered a victory. Although Spinelli and the European Parliament were bitterly disappointed with the outcome of the Single European Act, when put alongside the Parliament's Draft Treaty, the Single European Act has proved to be more dynamic and progressive than we at first thought. There has been a step forward on the path to democracy, a much bigger step than those opposed to a democratic Union — such as Mrs Thatcher and the Bruges Group — would have liked. A smaller step than the European Parliament was preparing to take, but a step none the less.

Parliament's two great strengths are that we have a plan and we have democratic legitimacy. We know where we want to get to and we have a map. A map which includes Utopia: a destination which we may never reach but which has some very desirable locations on the way — all of which are an improvement on where we are now. It is time to take another step on the path towards an ever closer Union.

Appendix

As an intergovernmental conference is the only way to reform the Treaties governing the European Community and because we are not likely, in the immediate future, to get the citizens of the European Community taking to the streets and demanding democratic control, the best way forward is by building consensus between European and national parliamentarians. It is our collective duty to democratise the Community for our electors. That process is already underway. A great deal of consensus already exists.

A Conference of Parliaments of the Community, the Assizes, was held from 27 to 30 November 1990 and brought together 173 members of national parliaments and 85 Members of the European Parliament. The following text was adopted by a very broad majority (150 for, 13 against with 26 abstentions);

FINAL DECLARATION

- having regard to the decision of the Presidents of the Parliaments of the European Community and of the European Parliament meeting on 20 September 1990 in Rome and to the conclusions of the inter-parliamentary conferences of the national parliaments' committees responsible for Community affairs and the European Parliament's Committee on Institutional Affairs,
- having regard to the draft Treaty of 14 February 1984 establishing the European Union and the resolutions adopted by the European Parliament on the basis of the Colombo, D. Martin, Giscard d'Estaing, Duverger and Herman reports,
- having regard to the memoranda drawn up by the national parliaments in preparation for this Conference,

A. certain that Europe cannot be built merely on the basis of discussions at governmental and diplomatic level, but that the Parliaments of the European Community must be fully involved in laying down the general direction it is to take,

B. whereas once the single market is established in 1993, the Community must adopt social, economic, monetary and environmental policies which give practical expression to the need for both social justice and economic democracy,

C. welcoming what has already been achieved, while seeking to re-model the Community into a European Union on a federal basis and to provide it with the appropriate institutions,

D. espousing the principles of pluralist democracy and respect for fundamental human rights,

E. proposing that, in keeping with the subsidiarity principle, only those powers should be conferred on the common institutions that are necessary for the proper discharge of the Union's duties,

F. regretting that the powers devolved on the Community and exercised by its Institutions are not subject to a satisfactory degree of parliamentary scrutiny,

G. whereas the extension of the Community's sphere of activity should be accompanied by a substantial reinforcement of democratic control,

Towards European Union

1. Is convinced that the creation of a large market without internal frontiers implies the creation of a monetary union governed by an autonomous central banking system, which should arrive at the issuing of a single currency; this development requires an Economic Union with an increase in economic, social and regional cohesion together with an enhancing of the Community's democratic legitimacy;

2. Takes the view that EMU must be achieved on the basis of the timetable and conditions agreed by the European Council in Rome on 27/28 October 1990;

3. Takes the view that the Community must finance its policy activities from its own resources; considers that the decision concerning the Community's own resources should be taken in agreement with the European Parliament and the national parliaments and that the financial provisions contained in the Treaties must be

thoroughly revised in order to ensure a more even balance between the two branches of the budgetary authority;

4. Takes the view that a Political Union comprising a foreign and security policy on matters of common interest must be established and that European Political Co-operation must be incorporated into the Treaty and into the Community structures;

5. Believes that the Community Treaties must provide for a common social policy and include adequate provisions for economic and social cohesion; this requires not only stronger assertion of the objectives in the Treaties but also decision-taking in these areas by qualified majority voting; further believes that, in addition to the financial and economic aspects, the social dimension must be strengthened and that a European system of concerted action involving management and labour must be set up;

6. Calls on the Community to pursue active policies to promote the equality of men and women in the fields of work, social and civil rights, education, participation in public life and access to political office at all levels;

7. Takes the view that regional policy must aim gradually to eliminate the disparities between the regions and considers that the resources at the disposal of the Community, notably the structural funds, must be reinforced;

8. Calls for provision to be made for every means of co-operation between the Community institutions and the regions as they are defined in the constitution or in law in the Member States;

9. Takes the view that the Community should be given additional competences in the field of the environment and that decision-taking in this area should be by qualified majority voting and that the Community must pursue a policy to preserve the environmental balance in the Community and the world; calls for Article 2 of the Treaty to be amended to express this objective which requires a process of sustainable development;

10. Calls for the inclusion in the Treaties of provisions to establish the idea of European citizenship, including the right for Community citizens to vote in European elections

in the Member State in which they reside; considers that respect for fundamental rights is the cornerstone of democracy; therefore requests the inclusion in the Treaties of the Declaration on Fundamental Rights and Freedoms adopted by the European Parliament on 12 April 1989 and the Community's accession to the European Convention on Human Rights;

11. Considers that a separate article on cultural policy should be inserted in the Treaty, stipulating that the cultural diversity and wealth of the Community nations must be respected and protected, particularly with regard to language;

Enhancing democratic legitimacy in the relationship between the Community and the Member States

12. Considers that the time is right to transform the entire complex of relations between the Member States into a European Union on the basis of a proposal for a constitution drawn up with the aid of procedures in which the European Parliament and the national parliaments will take part; takes the view that, in order to carry out the new tasks facing it at the monetary level and in external relations, the Community must transform itself into a European Union in order to meet the requirements of democracy, which entails adapting its Institutions and other bodies as follows:

— the Commission must progressively take on the role of the Union's executive;

— Parliament must play an equal part with the Council in the legislative and budgetary functions of the Union and its assent must be sought for all significant international agreements; it must be able to exercise democratic control, in the same way as the Council, over the executive bodies;

— the Council must be able to take its decisions by simple or qualified majority according to the circumstances; unanimity will only be required in the limited cases provided for by the Treaties.

13. Supports enhanced co-operation between the national parliaments and the European Parliament, through regular meetings of specialized committees, exchanges of information and by organizing Conferences of Parliaments

of the European Community when the discussion of guidelines of vital importance to the Community justifies it, in particular when the Intergovernmental Conferences are being held;

14. Takes the view that each national parliament must be able to bring its influence to bear on the shaping of its government's policy stances on the Community;

15. Takes the view that it is essential for the decisions taken by the Community to be implemented both by the Member States and the Community and calls on the Member States to take whatever legislative and executive action is required to ensure that Community legislation is transposed into domestic law on schedule;

Enhancing democratic legitimacy within the Community Institutions

16. Takes the view that the process of amending the Treaties must involve the assent of the European Parliament before ratification by the national parliaments, given that the European Parliament must be closely involved in the proceedings of the Intergovernmental Conferences;

17. Calls for the meetings of the Council, in its legislative role, to be open to the public and for it to act by majority voting except in connection with amendments to the Treaties, the accession of new member states and extension of powers;

18. Takes the view that the President of the Commission must be elected by the European Parliament, on a proposal from the European Council, by an absolute majority; that the President of the Commission, in agreement with Council, should appoint the members of the Commission, and that the incoming Commission as a whole should present itself and its programme to the European Parliament for a vote of confidence; believes that the Commission's term of office should start at the same time as that of the European Parliament; the same procedure should be followed if a new Commission has to be appointed during the parliamentary term;

19. Believes that, as regards the European Community's legislative powers, co-decision arrangements between the European Parliament and the Council must be devised and a right of initiative must be established in the event of the

Commission failing to act;

20. Believes that the European Parliament's supervisory powers must be enhanced and formally enshrined in the Treaties, and that the position of the Court of Auditors should also be strengthened;

21. Takes the view that the Commission should enjoy executive powers and the right to verify the application of Community directives by the Member States; emphasizes as well the important role of national parliaments in transposing directives into national law; takes the view that the Commission must enjoy the power to implement Community legislation, this to be co-ordinated with national governments and scrutinized by the Council, the European Parliament and the national parliaments respectively;

22. Draws to the attention of Member States, as contributions to reducing the democratic deficit, the need to take measures systematically that give wide publicity to their citizens of the proposals for legislation put forward by Community Institutions, as well as the need for their parliaments to ensure that their national governments and Ministers remain fully accountable for their policy and actions within the European Community;

Subsidiarity

23. Takes the view that any allocation of new powers to the Union must be based on the subsidiarity principle, i.e. the Union will only act to discharge the duties conferred on it by the Treaties and to attain the objectives laid down therein; where powers have not been exclusively or completely assigned to the Union, it shall act to the extent that the attainment of these objectives requires its intervention because their scope or their implications transcend Member State frontiers or because they can be carried out more effectively by the Union than by the Member States acting alone;

24. Takes the view that the subsidiarity principle must be enshrined in the preamble to the Treaties, and that, as regards interpretation, there must be scope for *a priori* political evaluation, while enabling the Court of Justice to confirm *a postiori* the extent of the powers of the

Community; considers that the principle of subsidiarity must be consolidated in amending the Treaties, and its substance clearly defined;

25. Takes the view that in the context of Community law, the adoption of measures governing of economic, cultural and social conditions should remain the responsibility of the legally constituted regions of the Member States whose constitutions contain provisions to this effect;

Relations with other countries

26. Stresses that although Community preference is to be respected, it must not make a fortress of the Community;

27. Considers that strengthening the Community would make it receptive to all forms of co-operation with European countries, ranging from free trade arrangements to accession for any democratic European state able and willing to accept the Community's objectives and responsibilities;

28. Believes, however, that the European Community must take account now of the welcome developments that have taken place in Central and Eastern Europe in recent months and that association agreements must be concluded with the new democracies, as well as with other European states wishing to strengthen their ties with the Community;

Relations with international organizations

29. Believes that efforts should be made with a view to collaboration with the EFTA institutions and that there should be ongoing co-operation with the Council of Europe;

30. Takes the view that the European Community has a role of its own to play within the United Nations, the Conference on Security and Co-operation in Europe, and the Atlantic Alliance, taking into account the particular situation of certain Member States, and that relations with the Western European Union should be redefined;

Relations with the developing nations

31. Takes the view that the European Community must continue to be permanently involved in the sustained development of all the world's nations, by giving absolute priority to measures to combat poverty and to aid for the least developed countries; in particular, it must strengthen

its contribution to the development of the underdeveloped countries with which it has ties for historical or geographical reasons or by virtue of co-operation agreements;

32. Submits this text to the national parliaments, the European Parliament, the European Council and the Intergovernmental Conferences; calls on the European Council and the Intergovernmental Conferences to take this declaration into account and requests that it be considered as an official document and that its conclusions be endorsed by the two Intergovernmental Conferences.

Elf Books

The Social Charter and the
Single European Market
John Hughes

With wide-ranging developments and changes set in motion in the course
of constructing the single European market, the needs of equity require a
rapid evolution of new norms of social and political principle and practice
to give substance to the Social Charter.
cloth 0 85124 523 4 £20.00
paper 0 85124 524 2 £6.95

European Union: Fortress or Democracy?
Michael Barratt Brown

Where is the way forward for economic and political development in the
East and the South, as they relate to the whole of Europe, and how are we
to overcome the plan-versus-market syndrome?
cloth 0 85124 520 X £20.00
paper 0 85124 521 8 £7.95

Against a Rising Tide
Racism, Europe and 1992
Mel Read MEP & Alan Simpson

1992 will bring enormous upheavals. How will it affect black people in Britain?
The authors offer pratical ways in which local people can combat racism,
setting their work in a European context.
cloth 0 85124 525 0 £20.00
paper 0 85124 526 9 £6.95

Whatever Happened to the
Peace Dividend?
The Post-Cold War Armaments Momentum
Marek Thee

A new arms race was underway before the Gulf War. The author sets out the
global drive for new high-tech weapons after the War, and makes clear why
Europe's arms industry must plan its own conversion.
cloth 0 85124 532 3 £20
paper 0 85124 533 1 £7.95

Europe and the Environment
Ken Collins MEP

If the European Community did not exist, it is arguable that we would have
to invent something akin to it to meet the environmental challenges we now
face in Europe. The President of the Parliament's Environment Committee
considers why.
cloth 0 85124 535 8 £20
paper 0 85124 536 6 £6.95

SPOKESMAN

Bertrand Russell House, Gamble Street, Nottingham NG7 4ET.
Tel: (0602) 708318